The Case for Letting Go

How to Find Balance in a World that Rewards Burnout

MATTHEW CAMPOBASSO

BROOKLYN WRITERS PRESS

BROOKLYN WRITERS PRESS
an imprint of the Aris Publishing Group, LLC

For permissions or bulk order inquiries:
publish@bklynwriterspress.com

ISBNs
978-1-952991-56-1 (e-Book)
978-1-952991-57-8 (Paperback)
978-1-952991-58-5 (Hardcover)

Library of Congress Control No.: 2025924422

First Edition

Printed in the United States of America

brooklynwriterspress.com

For every lawyer who thought they had
to carry the whole world on their shoulders.

For Luca, Gemma, and Bella
who remind me every day what's
worth carrying, and what isn't.

CONTENTS

Why I Wrote This Book

I didn't write this book because I had a clever idea. I wrote it because, a decade and a half into my legal career, I realized I was standing on the summit I'd chased for years, and I felt none of the air up there. I'd become the attorney I set out to be: evolved, trusted, useful. And yet, I felt hollow as a human being.

One afternoon around 4 p.m., in my home office between meetings, I finally heard the truth I'd been outrunning. Three monitors glowed: my email on one, Slack on another, and a document for our Board of Directors on the third. The desk was as clean and orderly as I kept everything, but I had been mistaking order for peace, and those are two very different things.

Blue-gray light slid through half-closed blinds and spread across the wood desk and carpet. The room where I'd sat ten to twelve hours a day, weekends included, for four years, went very quiet. My phone waited by the keyboard, exactly where it always did. In that silence, I knew with eerie certainty that if I didn't stop and take stock, another forty years would pass without making the changes I knew I needed. If I dismissed this moment and continued to neglect my body and mind, there would be no forward movement. That was the first honest bell.

There had been others. In 2018, just after I made partner at my then-law firm, I felt my heart thudding in a way I couldn't ignore. The cardiologist told me my heart was as fine and healthy as someone much younger, and then said the part that mattered: manage your stress. Migraines routinely started at the base of my neck, climbed to my forehead, and tried to carry me off. My fix was two Excedrin, some water, eyes squeezed shut, and then right back to the chair.

I slept, technically, but woke often with a racing mind and racing responsibilities. My calendar became my confession: sixty-plus hours per week, stacked meetings, and constant extraction. I was always “on” because I had unknowingly volunteered to be.

If you had asked me why, I would have given you the script I wrote as the oldest child: make sure your brothers are okay; keep the energy calm; clean up (literally and figuratively); head off conflict before it arises.

Later, law school poured concrete around that instinct. On day one of orientation, the dean of students told us, “We will change the way you think.”

They did, brilliantly, but somewhere in that rewiring, my brain took on a job it was never hired for: carry everything.

I can still feel the third quarter of a seventh-grade football game, my son's team, the Cary Junior Trojans, against Lake Zurich, mid-afternoon, when I looked down at my phone for work and looked up to a chorus of parents.

“Did you see that?”

“That was incredible.”

My son had made a textbook tackle. I nodded and smiled like I had seen it. My heart rate sped up with tormenting thoughts.

I did what I was supposed to, I showed up, but was I really there? In the car, he replayed the angle and the speed, lit up and proud.

“It was the best play you’ve ever made,” I said.

I meant it, although I felt sick that I’d missed it with my eyes. That’s the cost the résumé never itemizes: moments of joy you don’t get back.

The belief system underneath was loyal and irrational: I must be perfect. I must carry everything. I must make everyone’s lives easier, no matter the cost to me. I told myself that was my duty. I told myself that was what a provider does.

The counter-script arrived in pieces. One piece came to me at my desk, with soft music in the background, an Avett Brothers song reminding me to live without enemies, including myself. Another came in therapy, on a leather couch in a cool room, a clock ticking audibly on the wall, while I said out loud that I was doing exactly what I was told would make me successful, and my cup still felt empty. I left with simple homework: decide what I wanted next. I knew that meant looking at what had defined me in large part to that point, my career as an attorney.

I started with one tiny experiment: a list of what I can control. No grand gestures, no sabbatical, just sorting the controllable from the noise. The first practical change was the smallest and the strangest: I let an email sit. I began reading messages that implied urgency and asking whether urgency was truly present. If it wasn't, I gave myself time to think.

The quality of my work went up. So did the quality of my words. It became less about the speed of my reply and more about the substance of my response. Not everyone loved it. When the CEO said, "That was twenty minutes ago. You usually reply within a minute."

I said, "I'm trying to give myself opportunities to react with time instead of reacting immediately." It felt unprofessional at first. It turned out to be sanity-saving.

Boundaries followed. Some were visible: Do Not Disturb windows, "driving" and "sleeping" modes, calendar blocks that say Focus Time, Meditation, Morning Smoothie, School Pickup, Practice. Some were invisible: if it's not urgent at bedtime, it's for tomorrow. I stopped sprinting to the laptop because a notification chirped.

I told my team, "We've been programmed to be superheroes, but we're people who are members of a company. Strive to be great and aspire to be excellent, but also be human and realistic."

I started modeling the thing I was saying: not answering instantly, clarifying urgency, leaving my desk at 5:30 p.m. on a normal day without a fire drill, and then actually getting on the floor to play, or grabbing a controller, or reading a chapter book in bed with my seven-year-old, most recently Charlotte's Web, without my mind drifting back to the notification bubbles on my phone.

My mornings changed from reaction to ritual. I open my eyes. Wash my face. Stretch. Meditate. Do some yoga. I make my way into the kitchen for a smoothie with what feels like eighteen ingredients.

Vitamins. A glass of greens. Soft music. Controlled breathing. It sounds mundane, but it is quite the opposite. When I skip the ritual, the day feels like a tide that's already come in. When I prioritize it, the day starts on my terms.

The deeper work was identity, not scheduling. Old me in five words: *always ready to give everything.* New me in five words: *painfully honest about being human.*

That honesty led to apologies to others and to myself, not for doing too little, but for doing too much at my own expense and calling it noble. It led to a simple vow: I will not trade time with my children for a "win." Wins are everywhere. Their childhood is not.

Professionally, the work didn't get smaller; it got truer. I still lead, still carry weight, still answer hard calls. The difference is control without illusion. I no longer confuse an immaculate desk with a peaceful mind. I no longer treat my calendar like a verdict. I treat it like a tool.

A random Tuesday at 5 p.m. can look like this: I'm on the couch. The laptop is closed. Two cats (Mac and Ollie) are asleep next to me. The table is empty on purpose. There might be a Cubs game on, or music, or a favorite movie. That is "enough." Not because I've done everything, but because I've done what matters, and refused to let the rest colonize my evening.

If you want the cheaper version of all this: my job will take whatever I give it. No client or company will ever build a fence around my peace for me. That is my job. And when I do it, I'm better at the work that actually requires me, judgment, presence, and steadiness, because I'm a person again, not a machine that renders legal opinions on demand.

There's one more scene that matters. It's the stillness of the garage. It's cold. It's quiet. Every shift of my body makes the leather seat whisper. From the outside, I look like someone who has climbed his mountain. On the inside, I feel the dissonance clearly: the life the world sees, and the life I'm living. In that quiet, I hear the line I wish I'd whispered to my thirty-five-year-old self: It's not too late to change. Show yourself grace. Pay attention. Be honest. Do the work. Life is long enough to fix this.

And then there's the ordinary night that would have been impossible before: me and my three incredible kids, fast food and laughter with my youngest daughter (she is so funny), video games and a growing mess on the coffee table, a quick Target run (where my older daughter convinces me she needs more skin care), my son retelling a play with angles and speed like it's a movie he directed. Nothing headline-worthy. Everything headline-worthy.

That's why I wrote this book: to tell the truth about a profession I respect, and a life I refuse to outsource; to mark the turning points; to show the costs; to name the practices that actually help. Most of all, to hand one reader the essential first step I wish someone had handed me: stop and remember your identity isn't "lawyer." You are not obligated to fix everything. You're allowed to set things down. You're allowed to ask for help. You're allowed to be a human being, on purpose.

How to Use This Book

You're holding a book that isn't meant to be admired from a distance. It's meant to be worked with, thumbed through, argued with, highlighted, dog-eared, and revisited when life gets loud again.

Every chapter, what I call an Exhibit, is built to walk you through something I've struggled with myself. Think of each Exhibit as a case study in being human, where the facts are messy, the emotions are complex, and the verdict is never quite final.

Each Exhibit includes:

- *The Background*
- *Discovery Request*
- *Objections*
- *Ruling & Relief Requested*
- *Court Orders*
- *Settlement Terms*
- *Closing Argument*

The Background is where I lay out the story, the insight, the mistake, the lesson, whatever brought me to this particular piece of truth. Then comes the Toolkit: a set of structured, legally themed sections designed to help you apply the lesson to your real life. Use them sequentially, or jump to the one you need most right now.

BACKGROUND

This is the narrative, the part where I lay the facts on the record. You'll get context, candor, and whatever truth I had to drag out of myself at the time. Read it slowly. Let it hit. This is the "why" behind the work you're about to do.

DISCOVERY REQUEST

Your Reflection Prompt

This is where the flashlight turns on you. I'll offer a handful of questions intended to help you examine the facts of your own case.
No one is grading you. There are no wrong answers. But you'll get the most out of the work if you pause here and actually write something down, or at least sit with the question until it feels uncomfortably honest.

OBJECTIONS

What Gets In The Way

Every meaningful change runs into resistance. Sometimes it's fear. Sometimes it's ego. Sometimes it's the human tendency to cling to old stories like they're binding precedent. This section calls out the predictable pushback: the excuses, the mental traps, the emotional shortcuts. Think of it as clearing the courtroom before real progress can happen.

RULING & RELIEF REQUESTED

The Direction Forward

Here, I give you the core behavioral shift or mindset change the Exhibit is steering you toward. Not a miracle cure. Not a 90-day reinvention plan. Just a clear decision point: the relief I'm asking you to consider granting yourself.

COURT ORDERS

Your Tools

This is the practical, numbered, no-nonsense part. Simple actions. Small steps. Concrete tools. This is where theory becomes practice, and where letting go stops being an abstract idea and becomes something you can actually do, say, on a Tuesday at 3:15 when your blood pressure spikes.

SETTLEMENT TERMS

Your Letting Go Moment

Every Exhibit deals with something we hold too tightly: an identity, a fear, a belief, a resentment, a story we've outgrown. Here, you'll define what you're ready to release or renegotiate with yourself. It's the emotional exhale of the chapter: the part where you stop fighting the old contract and start drafting a new one.

CLOSING ARGUMENT

A Short Truth to Carry with You

Each Exhibit ends with a final, distilled takeaway: a brief reminder of what mattered most. Think of it as the line you return to when you need something simple, steady, and clear.

FINAL GUIDANCE

You don't have to read this book in order. You also don't have to treat it like a syllabus. You can work each Exhibit from top to bottom, or skip straight to the part that feels most relevant in the moment.

The only rule is this:
Bring Your Whole Self to The Page

Let the Backgrounds make you think. Let the Toolkits give you traction. Let the process be messy: real letting go always is. And when you need it, come back. The courtroom of your own mind is always back in session, and you always get another chance to rule in your own favor.

PART I

The Traps We Build

PART I

The Traps We Build

Law school didn't just teach you the law. It taught you how to think like a lawyer: habits of mind that win arguments but wreck your peace. You learned to control. To anticipate. To argue. To win. Somewhere along the way, those same skills became traps. The Exhibits in this section expose those traps: control, perfection, over-responsibility, and the ways your lawyer brain rewires you to treat life like a never-ending cross-examination. They show how we built our cages, and why we keep locking ourselves back inside. You cannot let go of what you haven't first noticed. This part is about noticing. Naming. Seeing the trap for what it is, not what it pretends to be.

EXHIBIT ONE

The Cult of Control

> *You're out of order! You're out of order!*
> *The whole trial is out of order!*
>
> —Arthur Kirkland [And Justice for All]
> *Al Pacino in full meltdown mode

BACKGROUND

The night the illusion first cracked was all fluorescent light and paper dust. We had a Temporary Restraining Order hearing at 8:30 a.m., and I was deep in the ritual: binders tabbed, outlines stacked, answers rehearsed for questions no judge had asked in a decade.

The night before, at 11:15 p.m., my phone lit up with a photo I'd taken that evening: my three-year-old and I lying in bed, his hair wild and curly, his hand across my chest. I'd gotten home late. Again. He'd whispered, "You here now?"

In the blue-white glow of that screen, I knew exactly what I was spending. Nine hours later in court, the judge, running hot from the prior case, cut us off, waved past the issue I'd over-engineered, and issued a narrow order that allowed for the injunction. We "won," but not because I controlled anything, or contributed anything material, if I'm being truly honest with myself. The weather shifted; we rode it.

That's the problem with control: it's a courtroom illusion. We never had it. We learned how to organize chaos with confidence and a citation. Control is a great strategy for document review. It's a garbage strategy for life.

It all begins with training. Law school doesn't teach surrender; it teaches issue-spotting, over-preparation, survival. We're conditioned to anticipate catastrophe and prevent it. Useful for liability exposure, lethal for a kid's T-ball game, a partner's feelings, or your own peace of mind. My first litigation assignment branded the reflex into me: make sure nothing blindsides us. I translated that and internalized it as control everything. I stayed late, convinced that one missed footnote would collapse a case and my career. The hearing turned on the judge's mood. No amount of redlines moves a barometer.

We grip harder. Do more. Stay longer. Leave no stone unturned. Meanwhile, the world is mostly uncertain. Trained to fear it, we spend careers trying to out-argue weather systems, calling it "zealous advocacy" while our lives trend toward a slow-motion nervous breakdown in a collared shirt.

Control is also a coping mechanism. It's a security blanket for people terrified of feeling powerless: over markets, courts, colleagues, kids, illness, and loss. We pretend we can finesse everything, preempt life with policy memos, treat heartbreak like a calendar invite. Spoiler: it doesn't work. The worst conflicts I've seen weren't about politics or parenting; they were about the inability to stop managing. Structure feels protective until it suffocates everyone else. Control doesn't preserve relationships; it strangles them.

You can see it in teams. Junior lawyers burn out not because the workload is impossible, but because they can't stop gripping it. They don't trust their colleagues, or time, or the basic truth that some outcomes are out of reach. They clutch the whole case to their chest, and when it falls apart, they mistake inevitability for failure.

The shift isn't abdication; it's triage. Know what you control (readiness, clarity, ethics, sleep), what you influence (expectations, coordination), and what you only witness (moods, calendars, luck). Prepare hard inside the first two circles. Hold the third lightly. Paradoxically, the work gets better. The room gets calmer. And the picture on your phone stops feeling like evidence against you and starts feeling like the reason you practice differently.

DISCOVERY REQUEST

What relationship, project, or habit has suffered most from your need to control-and how might it change if you trusted instead?

Legal Metaphor Break

i. Control is like a one-sided indemnity clause: you think you're protected, but you've created unmanageable exposure.
ii. You can't hedge every risk-not in a deal, not in love, not in your own mind.
iii. When control becomes your default, what disappears? Trust. Joy. Rest. Spontaneity. Humanity.
iv. You trade your breath for spreadsheets. Your presence for plans. Your peace for performance.
v. You stop living the life you have because you're too busy preventing the one you fear.

A Second Legal Metaphor Break

i. Control is like filing endless motions to compel after discovery has closed. You stay busy, feel productive, and still lose. Life (the judge) just stamps: "Denied."

OBJECTIONS

Objection no. 1
"But control makes me good at my job."

Sustained—in part.
Preparation matters. The world needs lawyers who bring order to chaos. But there's a difference between diligence and fear masquerading as competence. When control crosses the line, you stop being sharp and start being brittle.

Ask yourself:
Am I controlling this because it truly reduces risk, or because uncertainty makes me feel like I'm coming apart?

One is professional diligence. The other is personal fear dressed up in a power suit.

Objection No. 2
"If I don't control it, everything will fall apart."

Overruled.
Things fall apart anyway. Deals collapse. Cases get dismissed. Judges rule against you for reasons that have nothing to do with your preparation. Pretending otherwise just guarantees self-blame for what was never yours to own.

Confession: I once stayed up all night preparing for a board meeting, anticipating every question. I walked in bleary-eyed, armed with pages of notes. The chair's first question?
"Can we shorten your session?"
Control didn't save me. It just stole my sleep.

The Cost of Control

Buried under all that over-managing isn't just your peace-it's your identity. When I was most controlling, I wasn't creative. I wasn't funny. I wasn't even likable. I was efficient. Which looks great on a résumé and terrible on a tombstone.

The moments that still shine from my career aren't the ones I perfectly managed-they're the messy ones: the spilled coffee, the witness who went off-script, the late-night laughter that broke tension. Those are the stories worth carrying. Not the times I micromanaged risk into dust.

RULING & RELIEF REQUESTED

Ruling

The control is a legal fiction. The more tightly you grip, the less you actually hold.

Motion for Immediate Relief

Identify one area, professional or personal, where you will loosen your grip on this week. Write it on your docket under "Out of Jurisdiction." This is your first act of letting go.

Let's take a moment and talk about what your daily docket is. Throughout this book, I'll occasionally make reference to your Daily Docket for Peace. So it makes sense to explain what that is.

Your Daily Docket for Peace is a place for you to collect thoughts and reflections that arise while you explore this book. It's a place you can return to when you want to spend time with something I've asked you to share or an idea that you come across here that really resonated with you.

In its most simple form, it's a place for you to write drafts of the contract between who you are and who you are working to become.

SETTLEMENT TERMS

- Your duty of care ends where your control does.
- You are responsible for preparation, not prediction.
- You can deliver excellence without owning outcomes.

Write these into your Daily Docket for Peace.

CLOSING ARGUMENT

Your job isn't to prevent discomfort, fix everything, or to be perfect. Your job is to show up, do your best, and know when to say: *"That's outside my jurisdiction."*

COURT ORDERS

Conduct a Control Audit.

Practice
The Five-Minute Surrender

Review
Your Control Audit weekly & celebrate what you released

Repeat
The mantra: *Prepared, not possessed.*

This week list:
3 things you're trying to control at work
3 things you're trying to control at home
1 thing you know is already out of your hands

Cross out that last one and write:
NOT MY JOB.

Say it out loud if you need to. Revisit the list in seven days. Ask what shifted on its own anyway, and what it cost you to fight the tide.

EXHIBIT TWO

Perfection Is A Prison

> "The minute you start talking about what you're going to do if you lose, you have lost."

—Clarence Darrow
*Possibly the original king of overthinking.

BACKGROUND

The crack showed up as an extra space. We were filing an appellate brief in Wisconsin—300-plus pages with exhibits, more than a dozen copies already printed and mid-bind in office services. After thirty-six straight hours at the office (no change of clothes, just Dr. Pepper and adrenaline), I was finally going to leave at six.

Then the partner and I spotted it: a tiny, offending gap in the caption. I said we should live with it. He shook his head.
"How we do the little things is how we do the big things."

We fixed it. "Fixing it" meant stopping the bind, reprinting, and rebinding every single page. The copy room smelled like warm toner and melted plastic spines; blue painter's tape labeled piles:
"Vol. II – Appendix,"
"Authorities,"
"Tab 14."
Someone had written "DO NOT TOUCH" on a ream like it was a

museum piece. We pulled the plug, corrected the space, and watched a new run crawl out of the printer—page after page, the machine heating up like my first car's engine on a too-long road trip.

It was already dark. The building's HVAC clicked into its night rhythm. My inbox kept stuttering awake with read receipts and "thx." Somewhere between the second and third print cycle I did the math: those extra hours were coming straight out of my bank of time with a five-year-old who measured days by bedtime stories, and a one-year-old who fell asleep to the sound of white noise. Five hours debited, with no way to make them up.

By 10 p.m., we were loading eight bankers boxes onto hand carts, the partner in shirtsleeves, me in a wrinkled button-down that felt like sandpaper. We rattled through the lobby, past the security guard's two-finger salute, and pushed into the March air.

The sidewalk was crusted with old salt; our wheels chattered. At the UPS store, the fluorescent lights hummed like they were judging us. We asked for "Next Day Air—Early A.M."

The clerk, a college kid with a crooked name tag, whistled at the stack. "All this by cutoff?" We nodded.

He rolled his shoulders, printed labels, and we built a cardboard skyline of justice on the counter. I kept checking the wall clock like it could be negotiated. 10:42. 10:56. The final tape gun rip sounded like a starter pistol.

We left at eleven, not six. The street was empty except for our breath. We won the appeal, not because we murdered an extra space, but because we did the work that mattered and refused to quit when it got inconvenient. The substance carried the day; the effort made sure the substance arrived.

That's the distinction I wish I'd learned sooner. Aspiring to perfection can elevate the work; worshiping perfection warps it. One is craft. The other is fear in a tie.

Perfectionism sells itself as discipline. The voice sounds noble: *If I don't do this flawlessly, someone will be disappointed, angry, harmed, or think less of me.*

So, we become machines. We respond to the 9:17 p.m. email at

9:18 p.m. with flawless grammar and a clenched jaw. We triple-check commas, pre-solve outcomes that never occur, and call it "professionalism."

Often, it's a defense against uncertainty and judgment. The walls of that prison are familiar:

Guilt: *If I make a mistake, I've failed.*
Fear: *If it isn't spotless, I'll lose credibility.*
Comparison: *Everyone else is nailing this; why can't I?*
Control: *If I get it just right, nothing bad can happen.*

The job doesn't discourage it. Clients want certainty. The bar exam rewards precision without mercy. Senior lawyers model endurance, not balance. Each "perfect" outcome just resets the bar higher, until the line between diligence and obsession dissolves, and all that's left is exhaustion in a nice suit—and, quietly, hours you'll never get back with a five-year-old asking for one more page and a one-year-old reaching for your cheek to kiss.

DISCOVERY REQUEST

Where in your life has the chase for perfection cost you peace, and what would it look like to release that case?Answer honestly. The truth is admissible, even when it stings. Here's the reframe that keeps me out of the cage:

Aim for excellence, not flawlessness.
Excellence asks, *what moves the outcome?*
Perfection asks, *what might someone, somewhere, criticize?*

Define "done" before you start.
Must-haves: accuracy, clarity, ethics, timeliness.
Nice-to-haves: typographic nirvana. Time-box the polish pass.

Triage control. Control what's yours (readiness, reasoning, record cites). Influence what you can (team coordination, client expectations). Witness the rest (judicial temperament, calendar chaos). That Wisconsin filing taught both sides of the truth. Details matter; they signal respect for the court and the client. Fix the space. But don't pretend the space wins the case. What wins is substance, preparation, judgment, and, yes, two attorneys willing to push eight boxes on a cold night because the work and the standard deserve it. Perfection is a fine aspiration until it turns into fear. Then it stops serving you and starts owning you.

Legal Metaphor Break

Perfectionism is a non-compete clause you signed with your own soul. You agreed not to be human in exchange for approval, control, and a paycheck that never quite covers what it costs. It's time to breach the contract. Time to violate the terms. Time to be imperfect on purpose.

OBJECTIONS

Objection No. 1
"But isn't perfection why clients hire me?"

Sustained—with modification. Clients want excellence, not exhaustion. Excellence is competence plus humanity. Perfection is fear in couture.

Excellence says:
"I gave you my best work, on time, tailored to your needs."

Perfection says:
"I'll bleed myself dry so you never see I'm human."

And here's the verdict most lawyers never hear out loud: Clients can feel when you've sold your peace to buy their approval. Your presence is part of your performance.

Objection No. 2
"If I'm not perfect, I'll lose credibility."

Overruled. Credibility doesn't come from flawlessness; it comes from trust. You don't build trust by performing; you build it by being real. Mistakes handled with honesty make you more trustworthy—not less. The fear of imperfection always screams louder in your head than in the room.

The Toll of Perfection

Here's the math:

- Every extra hour spent sanding invisible flaws is an hour not spent living.
- Every mental replay of a "mistake" is a night of lost sleep.
- Every unnecessary round of edits drains a little more of your peace into a void that never says thank you.

The worst part? The standard keeps moving. You reach "perfect," and the next day it's "perfect plus one."

Perfectionism is a treadmill that speeds up the longer you run. I've watched brilliant colleagues quit-not because they couldn't hack law, but because they couldn't hack the silent, endless demand to be flawless. They didn't leave the profession. They escaped the prison.

The Moments That Matter

When I look back, the moments that mattered weren't flawless-they were real. The time I told a client, "I don't know, but I'll find out." The time I admitted to my team, "I'm overwhelmed."
The time I closed my laptop at 4:00 p.m. and went outside with my daughter instead of polishing one more email. Perfection would have stolen those moments. Presence gave them back.

And the mentors I remember? It wasn't their immaculate memos-it was their laughter after mistakes, their calm in the chaos, their grace when things went wrong. That's leadership. That's wisdom. That's balance.

Motion for Relief: The Intentional Flaw
This week, let one thing be imperfect-on purpose.

- Send the email without rereading it three times.
- Let the slide deck be "good enough."
- Show up to a meeting with no script-just presence and intellect.

Then reflect:

- What did I fear would happen?
- What actually happened?
- Did my world collapse, or did I survive (maybe even connect more)?

You'll begin to see the gap between fear and fact.

RULING & RELIEF REQUESTED

Ruling
Perfectionism is not proof of professionalism—it's evidence of fear.

Motion for Immediate Relief
Choose one place this week to practice imperfection on purpose. Call it your "Intentional Flaw."

SETTLEMENT TERMS

Write these lines on your Daily Docket for Peace:

- *Perfectionism violates my sanity.*
- *Excellence is diligence; perfection is self-punishment.*
- *Presence outperforms polish. Always.*

These are the boundaries between excellence and erasure. Write these three lines on your Daily Docket for Peace. Read them before you open your inbox.

CLOSING ARGUMENT

You're not a machine. Machines don't make mistakes—but they also don't laugh, learn, or love. And when they break, they get replaced. You are a person. People stumble. They repair. They grow. They surprise themselves. They matter. Stop chasing the fantasy of flawlessness. Start practicing the real art of being whole. The world doesn't need perfect lawyers. It needs human ones.

1. Practice the Intentional Flaw (This Week)
Let one thing be imperfect—on purpose.

Examples:

- Send the email without rereading it three times.
- Leave the slide deck at "good enough."
- Walk into a meeting with no script, just your mind and your presence.

Then ask:
What did I fear would happen?
What actually happened?
Did anything fall apart—or did things get easier?

You'll start seeing the gap between anxiety and reality.

2. Use the Ten-Minute Draft (Daily)

Pick one task you chronically over-polish. Give yourself ten minutes. Draft it. Fix typos only. Send it. Walk away. It will feel like stepping into court without your suit of armor. But you'll also feel more alive than the armor ever allowed.

- Use the Ten-Minute Draft daily for one task.
- Record the results in your Daily Docket: what felt risky, what actually happened.
- Replace the question "Was it perfect?" with "Was it honest?"

EXHIBIT THREE

The Counselor Trap

> *I suppose it is tempting, if the only tool you have is a hammer, to treat everything as if it were a nail.*

—Abraham Maslow [Law of the Instrument]

BACKGROUND

We were at a two-top in the lobby restaurant. The seasonal waterfall wasn't running, but the structure loomed over us. Every other table was empty. It was eerily silent. I still had my jacket on, tie loosened one notch, a notepad in my hand. Across from me sat a colleague and close friend—kind, meticulous, unflappable. He stared through me and said, almost casually, "I think my marriage is ending."

Before the word ending landed, training took the wheel. I held a legal pad. "Where will you live? You should start seeing a therapist—I can find you one. What will happen with the kids? Communication plan? What will you tell people?" Same cadence I use for a new client intake: timelines, contingencies, action items. He nodded politely at first, then I saw tears in his eyes.

"I didn't ask you to fix it," he said.
"I just wanted a friend."

There was the gavel. Same lobby, same suit, same brain I bill by the hour. But I'd forgotten I was human. Law school gave me a hammer so shiny I started mistaking every confession for a nail.

Vulnerability arrived, and I converted it into a project plan. The identity—counselor, problem-solver, stabilizer—had followed me to lunch and sat in my chair.

This is the trap. Somewhere between hypotheticals and your first real client, the title becomes the self. You stop knowing where your job ends. You don't show up as a colleague or friend; you arrive as outside counsel to the human condition. Two lies start running the show:

If I don't fix this, it will fall apart.
If I do fix this, they will love me.

They sound noble. They keep you functioning, mistaking usefulness for worth. Soon you're not just helping someone navigate a dispute, you're managing their emotions, summarizing options, emailing a PDF of next steps before the coffee cools. You don't hear fear; you hear gaps. You don't witness pain; you triage it. It looks like care. It lands as distance.

The costs are quiet and cumulative: relationships that feel coached instead of held; kids who stop bringing you small hurts because they don't want a closing argument; partners who learn to keep it surface because you turn a sigh into a seminar; colleagues who choose someone else for hard conversations because your empathy arrives stapled to a checklist. Admired for competence, avoided for comfort.

The profession rewards the reflex. Clients want certainty. Deadlines demand velocity. Courtrooms prioritize clean issues, not messy feelings. You're praised for being decisive, reliable, engineered for solutions. The muscle grows until it never powers down. You start scanning every room for problems to solve, like a security system stuck on "motion detected."

The shift wasn't heroic; it was procedural. I started where I should have started at that lobby table: scope. At work, I define matters; in life, I began defining moments. Three questions did it: "Do you want me to listen? Do you want advice? Do you want me to get involved?" If the answer was listen, I closed the file in my head. Short sentences.

Real silence. No timeline. If the answer was advice, I asked for a constraint: “What would be good enough right now?” If the answer was to get involved, I asked how my involvement could support or help. It kept the fixer from sprawling across someone else’s life without understanding the issue and the specific ask.

I also relearned a posture we claim in court and forget at lunch: witness, not weather control. I can offer clarity; I can’t guarantee outcomes. I can help name feelings; I can’t fast-forward them. Attention isn’t a lesser service; it’s the floor beneath any advice that might come later. Without it, solutions feel like verdicts delivered from altitude.

That day, I put the pad away. "I'm here," I said. "That's brutal." My colleague and I sat with the hiss of the wind blowing outside against the glass and the soft thud of the revolving door: two lawyers not lawyering for twenty minutes. Nothing was solved. We breathed. We hugged. The room softened by a single degree. Later, when he asked for ideas, we worked within his limits: one call, one boundary, one next step. Not a takeover. A handrail.

Fixing is part of the job. Making it your identity is how you lose the plot. The work needs your answers. The people around you, sometimes you most of all, need your attention.

DISCOVERY REQUEST

Where in your life have you mistaken helping for loving, and what might shift if you stopped giving counsel and simply gave care? This is a hard question. It’s supposed to be.

Legal Metaphor Break

In legal terms, you’re acting as both retained counsel and unsolicited amicus. You’re filing briefs in matters where you have no standing. You’re overreaching your jurisdiction, then wondering why you feel emotionally bankrupt. Let me be direct: you are not everyone’s lawyer.

OBJECTIONS

Objection No. 1
"But isn't being helpful a good thing?"

Sustained—with limitations. Being helpful matters. But when "helpful" becomes your entire identity, you lose sight of boundaries. You begin to equate love with usefulness, until your relationships run on performance instead of presence. And no one wants to be loved only for their utility-it's conditional, not connection.

Objection No. 2
"If I don't help, I'm letting them down."

Overruled. Let me share a case from my own record.
A friend going through a brutal divorce came to me. I launched into full strategy mode-legal options, financial angles, coping tactics. Midway through, he interrupted: "Matt, I just wanted you to talk to me." That was the day I realized: *sometimes fixing is failing.* Because fixing skips presence.

The Hidden Cost of the Trap

When you're always "on," people stop seeing you as a peer. You become a resource. A hotline. A lifeline. But not a person. It feels flattering-until it doesn't. Until you realize no one actually knows *you.* They just know your advice.

I learned this after years of being the default counselor in my family. Every decision-jobs, health, finances-ran through me. At first, I felt important. Later, I felt invisible.

I had built a role I couldn't step out of without disappointing everyone. That wasn't love. It was dependence.

And the cost wasn't just exhaustion-it was invisibility. When you're always the one with answers, no one ever asks how *you* are. They assume you don't break. They assume you're fine.
But you do break. Just quietly. Alone.

A Second Legal Metaphor Break
This trap is like over-billing. At first, it looks impressive-*look how much I'm doing!* But eventually someone realizes half the time entries were unnecessary. You weren't adding value. You were just padding the identity column.

Motion for Relief: The Counsel Pause
This week, when someone comes to you with a problem, pause before responding.

Ask: *"Do you want me to listen, or do you want help?"*
Then respect their answer.

It sounds simple. It isn't. Every instinct will scream *Fix it!* But if you sit through that discomfort, you'll discover something revolutionary: people don't always want counsel. Sometimes, they just want company.

Afterward, journal about what happened. Did the world collapse? Or did the relationship deepen?

RULING & RELIEF REQUESTED

Ruling
You cannot represent the world and yourself at the same time. Choose presence over performance.

Motion for Immediate Relief
Pause before fixing. Ask, "Do you want me to listen or help?" Then honor the answer.

SETTLEMENT TERMS

Write these three lines on your Daily Docket for Peace:

- *You are not counsel of record in every life you touch.*
- *Presence is often more powerful than advice.*
- *Listening is representation enough.*

These are your new boundaries—the difference between being needed and being known.

CLOSING ARGUMENT

If you spend your life being everyone else's lawyer, no one will ever know who you are beneath the role. You deserve more than being the world's counsel. You deserve to be yourself.

COURT ORDERS

The No-Brief Response
Choose one conversation this week where you give no advice at all. No strategies. No fixes. Just presence.

Try:

- *"That sounds really hard."*
- *"I'm with you."*
- Silence.

Practice the No-Brief Response in one conversation this week. Record what changes in your Daily Docket for Peace, the tone, the connection, the ease. Begin separating your identity from your utility. Feel what it's like to drop the robe, step out of chambers, and be human again.

1. The Counsel Pause (This Week)

When someone brings you a problem, stop your reflex.
Ask the scope-defining question:

- *"Do you want me to listen?"*
- *"Do you want advice?"*
- *"Do you want me to get involved?"*

Respect whatever jurisdiction they grant. This is boundaries as compassion, not withdrawal. Afterward, journal what happened:

- *Did the relationship tighten?*
- *Did the room soften?*
- *Did you feel more connected... or less burdened?*

2. The No-Brief Response (One Conversation)

Choose one conversation this week where you provide:

- Zero advice.
- No analysis.
- No strategies.
- No fixes.
- Just presence.

Feel what it's like to retire the robe for five minutes and just be human.

3. Separate Identity from Utility

Start noticing the moments when you slip into counsel mode:

- Offering solutions too fast
- Scanning for problems
- Interrupting with improvements
- Carrying emotional weight that isn't yours

When you notice it, mentally say:

"Not my matter."
This small cue interrupts a lifelong reflex.

EXHIBIT FOUR

Over-Responsibility Is A Form of Ego

> *With great power comes great responsibility.*
>
> —Uncle Ben [Spider-Man]
>
> *Not a lawyer, but if he were, he'd bill in six-minute increments.

BACKGROUND

The email with a subject line in all caps hit around 8:15 a.m.

CONGRATS TO THE LITIGATION TEAM ON A BIG WIN!

I was halfway through my double espresso, shirt wrinkled, when I saw my name high in the second paragraph, right after the partners, before the "and team." I reread it like a teenager replaying a voicemail. For ten minutes, it felt like someone had etched my face onto Mount Rushmore, right next to Lincoln. Then the emails from colleagues rolled in: "Incredible. Congrats." and so on.

I wasn't thinking about the client, the law, or the exhausted thirty-something who pulled 50 cites at 2 a.m. I was thinking, there it is. Proof. I'm the one who holds the line.

I grew up loving Superman. Cape, clarity, the whole savior kit. Somewhere between my first year of law school and my first trial team, "taking responsibility" braided itself to that cape. I told myself the load was mine because I could carry it, because I cared more, because standards matter. Sometimes that's true. Often, it's ego disguised as virtue. It's control wearing a polished tie. We call it reliability and service. Underneath, it's the quiet belief that if I don't hold it all together, everything will fall apart. That isn't just exhausting—it's arrogant.

You can hear the hero complex in the little moves. A junior associate turns in a solid draft; I "just tidy it up" and repaint the house. A colleague volunteers for a client call; I "hop on too" and answer every question first. A paralegal builds a flawless exhibit list; I re-sort it at midnight, convinced disaster hides in row 83. I tell myself I'm helping. Really, I'm monopolizing the oxygen. I've made myself the protagonist in everyone else's story.

Law doesn't discourage this. Clients want certainty. Deadlines reward velocity. The culture praises whoever "just handles it." Add an all-firm email with your name in bold, and the dopamine teaches you to audition for the cape in every scene. The problem is scale. Heroics don't scale. They create bottlenecks and brittle teams. They say to capable people, "I don't trust you, the process, or reality. Only me." The invoice shows up fast:

- **Burnout**: You're always on the hook because you keep hooking yourself.
- **Bottlenecks**: Everything waits for your review, so everything slows.
- **Talent rot**: People stop stretching because you'll "fix" it anyway.
- **Blind spots**: You miss strategy because you're hand-polishing footnotes.

I learned this the stupid way. A junior associate wrote a clean Motion for Summary Judgment—tight background, right issues, solid cites. I rewrote it line by line until it sounded like me and not at all more persuasive. The partner skimmed both versions. "You just spent six hours fixing something that worked fine." Translation: you fed your hero complex and starved your team.

The shift wasn't about abdicating responsibility; it was about right-sizing it. I started asking: What is really mine here, and what am I grabbing to feel indispensable? Sometimes, the answer was to lead. Often, it was to get out of the way, stay available, and let other people own outcomes. Credit began to flow down by default. Reviews got quicker and lighter: substance first, clarity second, no third pass to make it "sound like me."

The weirdest part? Results improved. Junior associates wrote better because they weren't writing for a rescue. And they got valuable experience every lawyer needs. Partners trusted me more because I stopped confusing control with quality. Clients got steadier (and less expensive) work because the system, not a savior, carried the day.

About Superman. I'm not him. Most days I'm not even Jimmy Olsen. I'm a lawyer with a team, a client, and a finite nervous system. Responsibility is sacred when it serves the work and the humans doing it. When it turns into a solo performance, it's just ego with billing codes. The all-company email still feels good; I'd be lying if I said it didn't. But the mountain I care about now isn't granite, it's a bench of people who can win whether my name shows up in paragraph two or not. That's the only monument worth etching.

DISCOVERY REQUEST

Where in your life are you confusing control with care and what might change if you stopped carrying it all alone? Don't rush it. The answer is usually humbling… and freeing.

Legal Metaphor Break
Over-responsibility is like drafting a joint-venture agreement where you give yourself 100 percent of the risk and zero percent of the upside. You think you're protecting everyone. You're just bankrupting yourself. When you shoulder it all, you rob others of their chance to carry their share. You disempower your team, your family, your partner. You don't just burn out-you burn bridges.

OBJECTIONS

Objection No. 1
"But isn't taking responsibility what good leaders do?"

Sustained—in part. Good leaders take responsibility. Great leaders share it. They trust their teams. They empower others to grow. Over-responsibility is leadership's evil twin-it looks like strength but smells like fear. It's not leadership. It's insecurity in a power suit.

Objection No. 2
"If I don't take it all on, things won't get done."

Overruled. That's the lie ego whispers. The truth? People rise when given room. I once let a direct report lead a board presentation. My stomach was in knots. Every slide looked like an accident waiting to happen. He crushed it-better than I would have. Why? Because he wasn't weighed down by my fear of looking foolish. Sometimes the best way to lead is to step back.

The Real Cost

Carrying too much corrodes relationships. At work, it turns colleagues into dependents. At home, it turns partners into passengers. Among friends, it builds a silent hierarchy-you as fixer, them as fragile. And the worst part? You like it. When you're the one solving everything, no one can criticize you. No one can disappoint you. No one can fail you-because you never gave them the chance. It feels safe. But it's lonely as hell.

A Second Legal Metaphor Break

Over-responsibility is like filing every pleading in a case yourself even when you've got a full team of associates. At first, it feels like diligence. Eventually, it's malpractice-against yourself.

Motion for Relief:
The Delegation Discomfort Zone

This week, delegate one thing that makes you twitch. Something you normally clutch like privileged material.

- Let someone else handle the deck.
- Let your partner manage the kids' schedule.
- Let your colleague run the meeting without your fingerprints.

Then sit in the discomfort. Don't swoop in to "fix." Don't redo it at 2 a.m. Just let it be.

Afterward, journal:

- *Did the world collapse?*
- *Did the outcome surprise you?*
- *Was your fear of imperfection bigger than the imperfection itself?*

RULING & RELIEF REQUESTED

The Ruling
Over-responsibility is ego masquerading as service. When you hoard control, you rob others of growth and yourself of rest.

Motion for Immediate Relief
Delegate one task that makes you anxious. Do not intervene afterward. Let it stand.

SETTLEMENT TERMS

Add these rules to your Daily Docket for Peace:

- True leadership distributes weight; it doesn't hoard it.
- Control shared is trust earned.
- Letting others carry part of the load is not weakness, it's wisdom.

These are your new rules of responsible leadership.

CLOSING ARGUMENT

Letting go of over-responsibility isn't just a work issue, it's an identity issue. If your worth depends on being the fixer, rescuer, or hero—

Who are you when you stop fixing?

That's the scary question. It's also the doorway to a healthier life. Because once you stop being everyone's safety net, you finally remember what it feels like to stand on your own two feet, and let others stand on theirs. Step back. Make space. Let others rise. You're not the whole team. You're one of the players.

COURT ORDERS

The Drop Test
Pick one responsibility this week-small but noticeable-and drop it entirely. Don't delegate it. Don't manage it. Just let it go undone.

Practice the Drop Test once this week.
Note what actually happened in your Daily Docket for Peace.
Replace the mantra *"I'll handle it"* with *"We've got it."*

You'll learn one of two things:

- Someone else will step in.
- It didn't matter as much as you thought.

Either way, you'll discover a liberating truth: you're not holding the world together by sheer force of will. Letting others carry part of the load is not weakness; it's wisdom. Add these to your Daily Docket for Peace as your personal leadership oath.

1. The Delegation Discomfort Zone (This Week)
Delegate one task you normally clutch like attorney-client privilege:

- Let a colleague run the client meeting.
- Let your partner manage the kids' schedule.
- Let your team handle the deck without your fingerprints.

Then sit in the discomfort, without swooping in later to "fix" it.

2. The Drop Test (Once This Week)
Pick one small responsibility you typically over-own, and drop it entirely. No delegation. No micromanagement. Just let it go undone. You'll discover you're not holding the universe together.

3. Replace the Mantra
Every time you feel the reflex to step in, tell yourself:
"We've got it."
Not "I've got it."

This subtle shift moves you from savior to teammate.

EXHIBIT FIVE

Your Brain on Law

> *You can't handle the truth!*
>
> —Col. Nathan R. Jessup [A Few Good Men]
>
> *Not a lawyer, but a warning label for every litigator.

BACKGROUND

The slide from preparation to over-preparation is quiet. One minute you're building a clean outline; the next, you've constructed a bunker. I remember a client meeting that should've been simple: scope the matter, set expectations, agree on next steps. I showed up with six binders, four potential timelines, and a contingency tree for scenarios that would require time travel.

I'd prepared to storm Normandy; the client wanted a weather report. We left with a plan (mine, not his), and I realized later I'd bulldozed the room with my anxiety, not my judgment. Same outcome we would've reached in twenty minutes. Far deeper costs: wasted hours, a spooked client, a tired team.

That's what happens when law school doesn't just hand you a degree. It rewires your brain. It changes how you think, argue, interrupt, order food, and even how you say "actually" or "correct" to friends who did not ask for your take on contract formation. This isn't necessarily bad. It's just… unrelenting. On my first day, the Dean of Students said, "In three years, your brain will be rewired, and you'll think like a lawyer forever. And some people won't like that." He wasn't kidding.

DISCOVERY REQUEST

Look at your own patterns with honesty, not argument. Where in your life is your analytical mind still trying to win a case that no longer needs a verdict? Sit with that. You may not love the answer, but you'll recognize it.

Law school is mental CrossFit. From day one, you're trained to:

- Argue both sides of everything.
- Anticipate disaster.
- Think in exceptions.
- Speak in clauses.
- Challenge every statement like a hostile witness.

You build analytical muscle fast and emotional coordination slowly, if at all. That skill set makes you formidable in court. At home? It makes you sound like a malfunctioning robot who's never had a genuine emotion.

I once felt like I demolished my brother in a casual political chat. I'm sure he still disagrees to this day. He offered a mild opinion; I came back with a three-prong argument, evidence, and a tone better suited for oral argument. The table went silent. He stared. My dad blinked. That's your brain on law.

You don't just hear what people say—you cross-examine it internally:

- *What did they really mean?*
- *What are they not saying?*
- *Could this become a liability later?*

You don't just prepare; you hyper-prepare. You don't just want answers: you want bulletproof, memo-ready, cite-supported certainty. When my daughter asked if she could go to a friend's lake house, I mentally drafted a risk memo:

- Transportation: medium risk.
- Supervision: low control.
- Mitigation: Phone GPS tracking?

She wanted a yes or no. That kind of thinking is great in a deposition. It's a disaster in a relationship. And at work, it's how you confuse preparing well with preparing more.

Preparing well means defining the question, gathering the key facts, pressure-testing the logic, and stopping. Over-preparing means trying to pre-live every possible tomorrow so none of them can surprise you. Same outcome, deeper costs: time bled from real priorities, jittery teams, clients drowning in detail, and a nervous system that never powers down.

Legal Metaphor Break

Practicing law sharpens your analytical muscles but atrophies your emotional ones. It's like becoming an elite litigator with zero experience in small claims court… of the heart. You start cross-examining your own feelings. You treat uncertainty like negligence and vulnerability like malpractice. This isn't moral failure-it's conditioning. But training is not destiny.

OBJECTIONS

Objection No. 1
"But isn't thinking critically a strength?"

Sustained—with clarification. Critical thinking is a superpower-when used in the proper forum. The problem is when you drag that forum into your living room. Your kid doesn't need a closing argument. Your partner doesn't want a deposition. Your friend doesn't need voir dire before telling you about their bad day. There's a time for litigation and a time for listening.

Objection No. 2:
"If I stop analyzing, won't I miss something?"

Overruled. You will always miss something. That's life.
The myth of total coverage is what drives lawyers into insomnia and burnout. You don't need 360-degree vigilance; you need 180 degrees of presence.

I once stayed up all night preparing for a settlement conference-every possible argument, every possible rebuttal. Not one of them came up. The opposing counsel cracked a joke about my coffee order, and the moment passed.

I had prepped for war, and peace broke out instead.

A Second Legal Metaphor Break
Your brain on law is like discovery that never ends. Every answer spawns three new questions until you're drowning in interrogatories that don't matter. Sometimes the most strategic move is to object.

"Overly broad. Unduly burdensome. Not proportional to the needs of this case."

The Cost of the Wiring

Eventually, this rewiring seeps into who you believe you are. You start to equate your value with being sharp, analytical, and on guard. You forget that being loved, trusted, or at peace doesn't require citation to authority. I've spent whole evenings overanalyzing a one-word text:

"Okay."

Was it agreement? Resentment? A coded cry for help?
Turns out it was… just "Okay."

That's the tax of an overtrained mind:
constant vigilance, zero rest.

Motion for Relief: The Thought Re-Frame
This week, pick one recurring stressful thought-the kind that loops like a bad fact pattern. Write it down. Then cross-examine it:

- Is this a *legal* problem or a *human* one?
- Do I need to analyze this-or feel it?
- Can I let this be unresolved?

If the answer is "no," pause. Ask again. This time, without your lawyer hat.

RULING & RELIEF REQUESTED

Ruling
Your legal mind is a gift—but it becomes a prison if you never leave chambers.

Motion for Immediate Relief
Identify one thought you'll stop cross-examining this week. Let it remain unresolved.

SETTLEMENT TERMS

Add these to your Daily Docket for Peace:

- *Critical thinking is a tool, not an identity.*
- *You can retire a thought without resolving it.*
- *Feelings are not evidence that need to be impeached.*

These are the rules that restore balance between the mind you trained and the life you're actually living.

CLOSING ARGUMENT

This is not about dumbing yourself down. It's about freeing yourself up. Law sharpened your logic. Now let it coexist with your intuition. Law made you a great advocate. Now become your own. Let your brain rest. Let your heart speak. Let your gut lead once in a while. You've done enough thinking. Try some feeling.

COURT ORDERS

The Two-Column Test
Draw a line down a page. On the left, list thoughts you treat like case law: detailed, footnoted, argued. On the right, list thoughts you'd allow to just exist if you weren't trained to dissect them. Compare the two. Notice how much energy you spend briefing issues no one asked you to litigate.

Practice the Two-Column Test once this week.

- When your brain starts drafting arguments, tell it: "Motion denied."

- Spend ten minutes each day doing something that requires no analysis-just presence.

1. The Thought Re-Frame (This Week)
Pick one recurring stressful thought, the kind that loops like a bad fact pattern. Write it down.

Then interrogate it with intention:

Is this a legal problem or a human one?
Do I need to analyze this, or feel it?
Can I let this be unresolved?

If the first answer is "no," ask again—this time without your lawyer hat.

2. The Two-Column Test (Once This Week)
Draw a line down the page.

Left column: Thoughts you treat like case law, detailed, footnoted, argued.

Right column: Thoughts you'd allow to simply exist if you weren't trained to dissect them.

Compare the two.
Notice how much of your energy goes to briefing issues no one asked you to litigate.

This is the emotional version of proportional discovery.

3. Ten Minutes of No Analysis (Daily)
Spend ten minutes each day doing something that requires zero intellect:

- A walk without a podcast.
- A shower without rehearsing arguments.
- Music without multitasking.
- Sitting still without drafting rebuttals in your head.

It feels oddly terrifying at first. Then it feels like relief.

PART II

Practicing the Pause

PART II

Practicing the Pause

Fast thinkers. Fast talkers. Fast responders. It's rewarded—even glorified. But speed comes with collateral damage: we forget the power of pause. This section is about reclaiming that pause. About learning to breathe between stimulus and response—to accept what we can't control, to grieve losses without immediately appealing them, to stop treating every ping in the inbox like it's a subpoena. The pause isn't weakness. It's a form of strength the profession rarely teaches and even more rarely rewards. The pause is where sanity sneaks back in. Here, you'll learn to slow down in a field that worships acceleration.

Remember that:

- *not every reaction is a response.*
- *not every loss is failure.*
- *not every silence needs filling.*

The truth is, pause isn't the absence of motion. It's the presence of awareness. Pause long enough, and you just might hear yourself again.

EXHIBIT SIX

The Breath Between Stimulus and Response

> *Between stimulus and response, there is a space. In that space is our power to choose our response. In our response lies our growth and our freedom.*
>
> —Unknown
>
> *Often misattributed to Viktor Frankl

BACKGROUND

Lawyers are masters of rapid response. Emails ping. Phones ring. Questions fire. Before your brain fully loads, you're already drafting a reply that's bullet-pointed, cited, and cc'd to four people who didn't ask. You don't respond, you react.

The profession trains us to be fast. Relentless. Unflinching. But every automatic reaction robs you of a conscious choice. If you never pause, you're not responding; you're running on autopilot. That isn't responsiveness; that's reactivity in a suit.

I learned this the expensive way, paid for in reputation points and lost sleep. One Sunday at 11:47 p.m., a board member replied to my email to the Board of Directors:

"This isn't enough." That was it. No context. No exhibit A.

At 11:48, my pulse spiked.

At 11:49, I had three paragraphs ready with a defense, citations, and a dash of righteous heat.

At 11:50, I stopped. I deleted the draft, closed the laptop, and said out loud, "This will look different in the morning."

The next day, the board member clarified she wasn't talking about my work at all. She meant the collective group's efforts described in my email. Had I hit send, I would've looked defensive and unhinged. The breath saved me. I couldn't control her unclear message, but I could control my next move.

That breath between stimulus and response isn't poetic fluff; it's a practice. It's the small, powerful gap between what happens and what you decide to do about it. It's the difference between sending a sharp email or sleeping on it; taking the bait or letting silence carry the weight; rehearsing a meltdown or choosing a measured reply. That space is your freedom. The problem? Most lawyers never find it. We're too busy, caffeinated, and addicted to urgency to ask: do I want to react to this or respond to it?

Law school rewarded speed. Firms glorify it. Clients expect it. We build reputations on being first out of the gate. But speed without space is a liability. It collapses curiosity, blurs facts with stories, and transforms simple moments into needless escalations. A witness pauses; we rush to fill it. A client venting sounds like an action item; we start solving. A stray comment in a meeting hits an old insecurity; we sharpen the elbows and call it leadership. None of that is discernment—it's habit.

Stoic thinking offers a counterweight: you don't control events; you control judgments and actions. The pause is where judgment gets inspected before it drives.

In practice, it's short and concrete:

Name the stimulus:
"Ambiguous critique at midnight."

Name the story you're spinning:
"Attack on my competence."

Ask one clarifying question or buy time:
"Noted. Can we discuss context at 9?"

Choose the smallest next right move. When you build that reflex, the room changes. Your emails shrink and land. Your meetings generate decisions instead of debris. Your team learns they don't have to match your adrenaline to get your attention.

Silence stops feeling like a vacuum you must fill and becomes a container that lets people finish their thoughts. You look calmer not because you're suppressing emotion, but because you're choosing a sequence:

notice → breathe → decide → act.

There's a reason we overreact: it feels safer. Reacting gives the illusion of control. Pausing admits uncertainty, maybe I don't yet know what this is. That's vulnerable. It's also powerful. The half-beat you take is a signal to yourself and everyone else: we're going to think first. It's remarkable how many faux emergencies resolve themselves while you're counting to ten.

The board email night rewired more than my thumbs. I started building micro-pauses into my day: one breath before I unmute; one beat before I reply-all; one lap around the floor before I draft the "final" paragraph. I set a two-minute delay on outbound emails; if I'm reacting, the draft catches me in the net. I write "What outcome do I want?" at the top of my pad before heated calls. None of this is dramatic. All of it is sanity on layaway.

These practices help me be deliberate and maintain perspective on what really matters and what I want to accomplish. When fear or negative emotion get involved, they can rob you of that perspective and turn your focus from outcome to ego. That's where things can go off the rails. You can still be fast. You just don't have to be first. Speed with space is judgment. Speed without space is flailing with punctuation. The pause isn't the absence of motion—it's the presence of awareness. Hold it long enough, and you'll hear the difference between your fear and your judgment. Then you can choose accordingly.

DISCOVERY REQUEST

When was the last time reacting made things worse?

What might have happened if you had simply taken a breath instead?

Don't overthink it. Remember it.

OBJECTIONS

Objection No. 1:
"But lawyers are supposed to be fast."

Sustained—in part. Timeliness matters. But speed without thought isn't speed, it's panic. Responding after a breath doesn't make you slow. It makes you deliberate, and that's what truly resonates with clients, judges, boards, teams, and even your own nervous system. The best lawyers aren't the fastest talkers. They're the ones who wait that extra beat and strike clean.

Objection No. 2:
"If I pause, I'll lose the advantage."

Overruled. Silence is leverage. In negotiation, in depositions, in leadership, I've watched silence reveal more than a dozen brilliant arguments. The pause isn't a loss of ground. It's an expansion of it. When you hold the space, people fill it.

RULING & RELIEF REQUESTED

Ruling

The pause is not a delay in progress. It is progress: the moment awareness takes the bench.

Relief Requested

Today, practice one deliberate micro-pause before replying to any triggering email or comment. Notice what changes, and consider how it might have gone if you'd just reacted. That's the lesson.

SETTLEMENT TERMS

Write these on your Daily Docket for Peace:

- The pause is discernment, not hesitation.
- Silence is composure, not weakness.
- One beat of delay isn't losing control, it's gaining it.

These reminders recalibrate your instinct to sprint.

CLOSING ARGUMENT

Space isn't indulgence. It's strength. That five-second breath or sixty-second pause might be the difference between escalating a conflict and dissolving one… between burning trust and building it… between a career built in reaction and a life built from choice. You've trained your mind to move fast. Now train your heart to stay grounded. Because in that space—between stimulus and response—you don't give up power. You reclaim it.

COURT ORDERS

1. The Micro Pause (Daily Start Point)
Before you respond to anything stressful:

- Breathe in for four
- Hold for four
- Exhale for four

Ask: *"What's the kindest response I can give myself right now?"*
This tiny sequence is a pressure valve for your entire life. It stops reactivity before it drafts the email you'll regret.

2. The One-Minute Rule (Once This Week)
When a moment spikes your emotions, a tone, a comment, a late-night critique, give yourself one full minute.

- Count to sixty.
- Breathe.
- Let your nervous system reset.

If you still feel the same, respond. If not, congratulations: you dodged a disaster by doing nothing. Log your saves. You'll start to see the pattern: restraint is often the smartest move you have. Track the moments you reclaim by keeping a simple log.
What triggered me?
Did I pause?
What changed?
What would have happened if I'd reacted instead?

Review weekly. This is evidence that your nervous system doesn't have to run your calendar.

EXHIBIT SEVEN

Accepting the Uncontrollable

> *Suffering arises from trying to control what is uncontrollable, or from neglecting what is within our power.*

—Epictetus

*Greek Stoic philosopher born into slavery.

BACKGROUND

Let's talk about control. Again. We've already pulled back the curtain on its illusion; now we walk into the part lawyers resist most: acceptance. Not the polite "It's fine" while you quietly scheme a workaround, but the kind that feels like surrender but is actually strength. The kind that looks at a situation (messy, unfair, unresolved) and says, with a clear spine: This is outside my jurisdiction.

Acceptance understands that not everything deserves your red pen, your strategy, or your emotional bandwidth. Trying to control what can't be controlled doesn't make you powerful. It makes you miserable.

Law conditions us to believe nothing is final until we say so. Appeal it, amend it, restructure it: movement equals progress. That bias keeps clients alive in hard cases. It also turns ordinary life into an endless motion calendar. We start treating the weather like it owes us briefing. Acceptance cuts across that reflex. It's not a retreat; it's a reclassification. Some matters belong to reality, not to you.

It's important to remember the current is stronger than you are. There will be clients you can't save, deals you can't close, people you can't change, partners who don't like you, kids who don't listen, judges who don't care. Your brain will whisper, *If I just try harder, I can fix this.* Your ego will answer, *If I let go, I'm weak.*

The truth: you are not the current. You are the boat. You can steer. You can trim the sail. You can read the water. But you do not command the river. The longer you fight it, the more energy you bleed. The moment you align with it, you move, not because the world finally obeyed you, but because you stopped insisting it shouldn't be what it is.

Years ago, I worked on an acquisition where the math never made sense. From the start, the fundamentals wobbled: valuation assumptions that needed a fairy tale, synergies that lived in slides but not in cash. We redrafted the term sheet a dozen times, adding cleverness that drifted toward delusion: collars, ratchets, governance contortions, "bridge" ideas to nowhere. I kept saying we were one tweak away. The owners' optimism thinned into euphemism. Everyone else read the wall; I kept rewriting it.

Ninety days in, it was midnight at my desk. Spreadsheets contradicted each other like competing witnesses. Another attorney messaged: "If it only works in the model, it doesn't work." I nodded, opened a clean document, and kept moving commas on a house with no foundation. When the deal collapsed (the seller walked, and financing evaporated), I blamed the exhaustion on the loss. Later, I realized I wasn't tired from the outcome; I was tired from refusing it sooner. The deal needed to die. I didn't know how to let it.

Acceptance landed in the quiet after. Not a moral, not a technique: just a recognition that some endings are not failures but facts. The work shifted from forcing life into my plan to honoring what the facts would permit: preserving relationships instead of burning them, capturing what diligence could still teach, telling a clean story of "why not" that respected everyone's time. A month later, a saner opportunity came through the same channel, likely only because the ground wasn't scorched.

. . .

Acceptance isn't approval. It isn't apathy. It's acknowledgment. It's the moment you stop cross-examining reality and start collaborating with it. It sounds like: The judge won't move the schedule. This witness won't improve with another prep. This revenue is fantasy. From there, choices multiply. Without acceptance, you throw good time after bad, defending a narrative that needs you more than your client does.

There's humility in this posture, and a particular kind of courage. To accept that you are the boat is to release the fantasy that competence guarantees outcomes. It doesn't. Competence gives you a better boat. Wisdom keeps you from rowing yourself to pieces against a current that doesn't care about your boat.

If control is the story that says, "The world will yield if I try hard enough," acceptance is the counter-story: "I will meet the world as it is, and choose accordingly." One is loud and impressive. The other is quiet and sane. Only one lets you keep your strength for the places it can be impactful.

DISCOVERY REQUEST

What are you still trying to control that's clearly outside your jurisdiction, and what would freedom look like if you let it drift? Write it if you can. Name it if you can't. In any case, face it.

OBJECTIONS

Objection No. 1:
"But if I accept it, doesn't that mean I failed?"

Overruled. Acceptance is not failure. Acceptance is recognition. Lawyers cling to un-winnable jobs, cases, and relationships because the optics of "quitting" terrify them. But refusing to accept a fact doesn't change the fact. Courage isn't fighting every battle. Courage is knowing which battles are yours to fight at all.

Objection No. 2:
"But what if it could have worked?"

Sustained—but irrelevant. Maybe it could have. Maybe it couldn't. Living in "what if" is how lawyers burn themselves down to the studs. Acceptance is how you step out of fantasy and into clarity. It's not about giving up—it's about putting down the sword when the war is imaginary.

RULING & RELIEF REQUESTED

Ruling
Acceptance is not surrender. It is jurisdictional clarity: you cannot fix what's outside your authority.

Relief Requested
Choose one situation this week that is clearly out of your control. Write "Dismissed" next to it. Read it aloud.
Then, let it go.

SETTLEMENT TERMS

Add these to your Daily Docket for Peace:

- You can care without controlling.
- You can release without failing.
- You can accept without apathy.

These are the doctrines of surrender—not weakness, but wisdom.

CLOSING ARGUMENT

Acceptance doesn't mean you don't care. It doesn't mean you're weak. It means you've stopped fighting gravity. Life rarely obeys your outline. That's not a flaw in your planning—that's the nature of being human. Letting go isn't the end of effort. It's the beginning of sanity. This isn't just the practice of law—it's the practice of living. And the sooner you release what was never yours to command, the sooner you regain the strength to influence what is.

COURT ORDERS

1. The Jurisdiction List (This Week)
Write down three things weighing on you. Next to each, *ask*:

Is this within my control?
If the answer is no, write: Dismissed.

This isn't abandoning responsibility. It's recusing yourself from cases that were never yours to argue.

2. The Bench Trial (Once This Week)
Pick one uncontrollable situation—a stalled deal, a stubborn person, a slow process. Then, imagine yourself as the judge.

No arguments. No evidence. No persuasion.

Just the ruling:
"This is outside my control. Case closed."

Say it out loud. Feel the verdict settle in your body. That sensation? That's release.

3. Rewrite the Internal Script
Every time your mind reopens a closed case, replace:

"What if I lose control?"
with:
"What if I find peace?"

This is the doctrinal flip, choosing peace over panic.

EXHIBIT EIGHT

When the Case is Lost

> *I fought the law, and the law won.*
>
> —Bobby Fuller
> *and, eventually, every lawyer

BACKGROUND

We prepped for months. Every exhibit tabbed. Every witness rehearsed. Every line of questioning mapped, color-coded, and rehearsed until the rhythm felt inevitable.

In court, under lights two degrees harsher than necessary, the plan held, until it didn't. On cross, a key witness who'd been steady in every prep wobbled. A small inconsistency grew teeth. Opposing counsel pressed. The witness corrected, then contradicted the correction. You could feel the jury's attention tilt, subtle at first, then unmistakable. In less than an hour, the case we'd engineered began shedding screws.

When we adjourned, we told ourselves the comforting half-truths: redirect will stabilize it; the jury instruction will reset the frame; closing will stitch it back. It didn't. We lost. Walking out of court, I felt hollow and overheated, like my body had kept the lights on but unplugged the furniture. My reflex was to fix the feeling: write the post-mortem, translate the ache into "lessons learned," convert grief into productivity. That night, in a hotel room with a view of a parking lot I don't remember, I finally cracked. Not because we lost, but because I'd refused to admit to anyone, myself included, that the loss mattered. The grief had nowhere to go, so it settled into my chest like wet concrete.

Here's the part we skip past in our profession: no matter how sharp you are, how long you prepare, or how tightly you white-knuckle the outcome, some cases, deals, and relationships still collapse. You lose the motion. You miss the deadline. The client ghosts. The deal implodes. The relationship ends. The thing you swore would never happen… happens anyway. You did everything you could, but the world, and sometimes the other side, had different plans. Now what?

Law's sanctioned answer is velocity. File the appeal. Draft the memo. Rework the strategy deck. Pretend you didn't just pour eighty hours and a chunk of your sanity into something that evaporated. There's no time to process. No space to grieve. Keep moving. Keep winning.

We're brilliant at arguing. We're awful at mourning. No one teaches you how to sit in a loss without reframing it, without spinning it into a tidy "growth moment," without converting it into a parable for LinkedIn. The simple, honest words are: that hurt. That *mattered.* That's not how I wanted it to go. These words feel dangerous, like professional malpractice.

But the myth underneath our speed is louder than the loss: if we work harder, think faster, care deeper, we can prevent bad outcomes. That isn't law. And it is definitely not life. That's magical thinking with a J.D. Courtrooms are human rooms. Boardrooms are human rooms. Homes are human rooms. In human rooms, loss shows up uninvited. Some witnesses collapse. Some judges don't care. Some markets turn while you're asleep. Some people choose an ending you didn't vote for. The goal isn't to erase that truth; it's to carry yourself through it without confusing the verdict for your value.

Losing well doesn't mean pretending the sting is insight. It means letting the sting be sting. It looks like boxing exhibits without rewriting history to absolve your ego. It sounds like telling the team, *we did the work; the result is the result.* It feels like walking to the elevator without dragging the wreckage home to your partner, your kids, your sleep.

You are not the outcome. You are the person who stood there and did the craft as well as you could, and who will stand there again.

What I remember most from that trial isn't the ruling; it's the moment after. Someone made a dumb joke while we broke down the war room and we laughed a little too hard because our bodies needed a release valve. In the car to the airport, no one tried to re-litigate the day. At some point, the first real breath landed, one that didn't taste like adrenaline. The loss didn't vanish. It took its seat. And when it did, capacity returned: for the next case, for the next client, for my own life outside the building.

There's a particular dignity in acknowledging that some endings come no matter how careful you are, while still honoring the work that tried to make them otherwise. It isn't resignation. It's proportion. You stop treating every outcome like a vote on your worth. You stop bargaining with reality to spare your pride. You let the loss matter and then you let it move. That's how you keep practicing without turning yourself into collateral damage.

DISCOVERY REQUEST

What loss have you refused to feel—and what would healing look like if you finally let it take the stand? That's the question this Exhibit is asking you to stop dodging.

OBJECTIONS

Objection No. 1
"But losing means I wasn't good enough."

Overruled. Skill and outcome are not perfectly correlated. Even the best lawyers have losses in their record, often some of their most defining, most clarifying ones. Sometimes you were out-lawyered. Sometimes the judge had a bad morning. Sometimes the facts were simply against you. Losing doesn't mean you weren't good. It means you were human.

Objection No. 2
"If I don't fix it, it'll define me."

Sustained—with modification. Yes, unprocessed loss can define you. But fixing isn't the same as feeling. Fixing is a sprint to control the narrative. Feeling is letting the truth land so it can move through you, not calcify inside you. If you skip the feeling, the pain doesn't disappear; it goes underground and cross-examines you later.

RULING & RELIEF REQUESTED

Ruling
Loss is not the opposite of success. It's proof that you were in the arena.

Relief Requested
Write one page identifying and describing a professional or personal loss you've carried for far too long. Then rest your case. This is not closure—it's honesty.

SETTLEMENT TERMS

Add these to your Daily Docket for Peace:

- You can lose without being a loser.
- Feeling is not weakness; it's evidence of care.
- Every good lawyer knows when to rest their case.

These are the doctrines of grace, the antidote to self-punishment.

CLOSING ARGUMENTS

You are allowed to be wrecked and still whole. You are allowed to break down without breaking apart. You are not your wins. You are not your losses. You are the one who keeps showing up—again and again and again. Loss doesn't diminish you. Loss reveals you. And the person revealed is still worthy, still capable, still here.

COURT ORDERS

The Brief for the Broken (This Week)
Write a one-page closing argument for a professional or personal loss you're still carrying.

Include:

- The facts
- The effort
- The pain
- The acknowledgment

Then, rest your case. Burn it, save it, frame it—doesn't matter. What matters is that you finally put the loss on the record.

1. The 24-Hour Rule (Next Time You Lose)
When you take a hit, case, deal, relationship, whatever, grant yourself twenty-four hours to feel it fully.

No reframing.
No silver linings.
No appeals.
Just truth.

This hurts. After twenty-four hours, shift to: What's next?
Not as avoidance, as balance: mourning followed by motion.

2. The Language Shift
Replace:
"I failed" with
"That mattered."

It changes everything. The shame dissolves. The humanity stays.

EXHIBIT NINE

Not All Emails Deserve a Response

> *Worry never robs tomorrow of its sorry, it only saps today of its joy.*
>
> —Leo Buscaglia

BACKGROUND

I was court-side on a Saturday, in the kind of rec-gym where the lights hum and the floor smells like industrial cleaner. My oldest daughter brought the ball up, chin high, legs a little wobbly with adrenaline.

My phone buzzed:

"URGENT quick thoughts?"

I glanced down, thumbed a reply between possessions, because that's what professionals do, right? Be reachable. Be fast. Be indispensable. I hit send. At that exact moment, she pulled up from downtown. Net, clean. The crowd popped. I caught the echo of it, the tail end of her grin, and the look she shot toward the bench: did you see?

I didn't. I saw just before and just after, but not the second that mattered most. I'd been busy proving I cared about work.

That day, I made myself a promise: some emails deserve to rot in peace.

Here's the thing the profession won't admit out loud: we treat the inbox like litigation triage: as if every subject line is a subpoena and every silence is malpractice. It's not. It's just email. The 10:07 a.m. "Did you see my email?" from the same person who sent it at 10:02 a.m. is not a four-alarm fire; it's a habit.

Threads breed overnight because the medium rewards reflex, not thought. And somewhere along the way, we let our response time become a proxy for our worth.

- *Respond fast? You're committed.*
- *Respond instantly? You're elite.*
- *Respond later than expected? You okay, buddy?*

It's absurd. You didn't go to law school to become a glorified customer service rep with a bar card. You are not a public utility. You are allowed, and often obligated, to pause before replying. Or not reply at all.

The inbox is an identity crisis dressed as productivity. We tell ourselves we're being responsive, but often we're just being reactive, rewarding the loudest ping and training colleagues and clients to expect our consciousness on demand. We flood the zone with half-thought answers, cc four people who didn't ask, and call it diligence. Then we sit there at 11:43 p.m. with a tight jaw and a hollow chest, wondering why we feel both important and empty. The email won; the work lost.

And this approach has a cost. Real work, the kind that changes cases, steadies clients, and leads teams, requires uninterrupted thought. Presence with your people requires full attention. The constant twitch to check, to answer, to prove you're "on it" slices both to ribbons. You end up living in the shallow end of everything: half-parenting, half-lawyering, half-sleeping, wholly depleted.

There's also the math no one wants to do. Many emails aren't requests for legal judgment; they're anxiety looking for a host. Some are status theater ("circling back," "bumping this," "quick nudge"): a dance we all perform because we're afraid of being the one who slows the dance down. Some are just noise. Treating all of them as sacred collapses your ability to tell the difference between signal and static.

This isn't a manifesto for rudeness. It's a call for discernment. Not every message merits the same calorie burn. Some need urgent, thoughtful response. Some need a same-day acknowledgment and a later answer. Some need a question: what's the actual decision here? And some need absolutely nothing. Silence is not contempt; sometimes it's clarity. If the content doesn't advance a matter, protect a relationship, or prevent harm, why are you giving it your Sunday?

The courtside miss wasn't just a parenting fail; it was a professional tell. I'd confused being constantly available with being truly effective. I was letting other people's clocks set my value. That's not service. That's surrender. The pause between an email and your reply is where judgment lives: What is this, really? What outcome do I want? What deserves my best attention right now? When you reclaim that gap, something shifts. You start writing fewer, better messages. Meetings replace flurries. Clients get calmer because you are. And you start being present for the moments that don't repeat.

My daughter still takes long shots. I see more of them now. The phone still buzzes. Some of those messages still get an answer, soon and clean. Others wait. A few vanish into the sediment of the thread, unrequited and un-missed. The work hasn't suffered. The work is better. And the look a kid gives when she knows you saw her make the shot? No email on earth deserves to outrank that.

DISCOVERY REQUEST

What does your inbox reveal about your boundaries, and what might peace look like if you stopped trying to win the email war? Boundaries aren't built in your calendar. They're built in your choices.

OBJECTIONS

Objection No. 1
"But if I don't respond, I'll look unprofessional."

Overruled. Professionalism isn't measured in reply speed. It's measured in reliability and substance.

You can be thorough without being tethered. Silence doesn't make you careless. It makes you selective. Replying "Thanks" to a twelve-person chain isn't professionalism; it's muscle memory.

Objection No. 2
"But what if it's urgent?"

Sustained—in part. Yes, some emails require immediate attention. But the problem isn't the occasional emergency, it's treating every message like it's stamped TIME SENSITIVE in blood. If everything is urgent, nothing is. Discernment is the job. Not speed. Not compulsion. Discernment.

RULING & RELIEF REQUESTED

Ruling
Your inbox is not a courtroom.
You are not on the clock for every ping.

Relief Requested
Practice one Strategic Non-Reply today. Let an email sit unanswered. Observe the world continue turning. That's your first reclaimed breath.

SETTLEMENT TERMS

Add these to your Daily Docket for Peace:

- Your inbox is not your identity.
- Responsiveness is not the same as responsibility.
- Silence is a valid response, sometimes the smartest one.

These are your Email Clause, your new rules of reasonable silence.

CLOSING ARGUMENT

You will never reach Inbox Zero and stay there. It's not a finish line. It's a fantasy. The inbox is a living organism that feeds on guilt. Stop feeding it.

Not everything deserves your time.
Not everything deserves your energy.
Not everything deserves you.

- Choose presence over ping.
- Choose discernment over reflex.
- Choose your daughter's long shot over someone else's anxiety.

Some emails deserve to rot in peace.

COURT ORDERS

1. The Strategic Non-Reply (Today)

Identify five emails this week that do not require a response.

- Read them.
- Acknowledge them internally.
- Then do nothing.

No "*Thanks*."
No "*Got it.*"
No "*Looping back.*"
No "*Quick thoughts below.*"

Let silence be the strategy.
Sit in the discomfort. Feel the twitch. Then watch it pass. That's discipline disguised as stillness.

2. The Inbox Audit (Daily for One Week)

At the end of each day, choose one chain you wish you hadn't replied to.

Ask:

- *What did my response add?*
- *Did it change anything?*
- *Or did it just feed my compulsion?*

Use the data.
Recalibrate.

Over time, you'll realize silence often wins arguments you never needed to enter.

3. Update the Mantra

Replace:
"I need to respond." with
"I'll respond if it's worth it."

Worth is the metric, not speed. Not fear. Not guilt.

EXHIBIT TEN

You Are Not Your Wins

> *That's the difference between you and me:*
> *you wanna lose small, I wanna win big.*

—Harvey Specter [Suits]

*Peak lawyer swagger minimal emotional maturity.

BACKGROUND

It fell apart on a Wednesday, the kind of day that already felt over-lit. We'd spent weeks inching two angry parties toward a settlement number everyone could live with. Settlement term sheet drafted. Mediator cautiously optimistic. I'd rehearsed the last-mile script in my head, concessions here, face-saving language there, the soft landing a good settlement deserves.

Then, at 4:12 p.m., opposing counsel called: "My client's out." No explosion, no villain monologue. Just a clean walkaway.

My first thought wasn't about litigation risk or budget impact. It was a punch to the ribs: *They're going to think I failed. I don't belong at this table.* No one said that. Leadership's response was brisk and sane:

"Tough break. We'll reset."

But internally, I'd already held the trial and read the verdict. I didn't just lose a settlement. I lost a version of myself. If I wasn't the person who could get this closed, who was I?

Let's be honest: lawyers love to win. We need to win. We were raised on gold stars, LSAT percentiles, and being the kid teachers asked to "help the others catch up." Then came law school. Then firms. Then titles, bonuses, verdicts, "Great work" from people whose approval we crave more than we admit. Winning became the measure. Then the identity. We didn't just succeed; we became our success. We didn't just win; we were the win. That's where the trouble starts.

Somewhere along the way, we internalize a formula that looks airtight on paper and destroys us in practice:

If I win, I'm valuable. If I lose, I'm worthless.

It doesn't feel like a belief; it feels like gravity. It drives late-night outlines and eleventh-hour brilliance. It also builds a trapdoor under your feet. The moment a verdict tilts wrong, a client ghosts, or a settlement dies at the altar, you don't just feel disappointment, you feel erased. That's not resilience. That's a toxic merger of identity and performance.

After that collapse, I did what lawyers do: I tried to out-argue the feeling. I drafted a memo on leverage shifts and last-minute anchoring. I assembled a strategy focusing on settlements that died and later resurrected. I reframed the narrative to anyone who asked. None of it touched the thing that hurt, because the thing that hurt wasn't the outcome. It was the private math I'd been running since my first year of law school grades were released: outcomes prove I belong; losses prove I don't. The math felt empirical. It was just loud.

The profession doesn't help. Every evaluation is based on results. Every bio reads like a scoreboard: "secured favorable settlement," "obtained dismissal," "defeated class certification." Clients open with, "What's your trial record?"

We learn to curate wins, to perform certainty, to make the highlight reel look like the whole film. But life isn't litigation, and you're not a walking résumé. You can be proud of your work without being your work. You can feel successful even when the other side walks. You can be enough regardless of how anyone else scores the game.

What makes this so hard to untangle is that winning works…until it doesn't. It moves careers. It buys credibility. It also shrinks you to the surface area of your last outcome.

You become volatile to every mediator's eyebrow raise; every counteroffer typed with too many zeros. Your nervous system turns into a market chart, spiking and crashing with each email. You start optimizing for the next notch instead of the next right move. You over-sweeten a term to keep the "win" alive when "no deal" would be wiser. You overwrite a junior associate's draft because sounding like you feels safer than letting the team own the moment. The work gets tighter and thinner at once.

When that settlement died, the silence afterward taught me more than any victory lap. I kept expecting shame to move me to work harder, be sharper, to fix it. Instead, it just made everything small. The room, the team, the options. Shame wants a cape; craft wants a chair.

Craft says: did you prepare well, judge risk honestly, keep faith with facts and ethics, make room for your team to do their best work? If yes, then the outcome is data, not identity. Settlement or trial is a path, not a personality test.

Winning still matters. Clients deserve our best shot at resolution. But the identity we strap to winning needs a smaller chair. When victory is the only mirror you recognize yourself in, every walkaway looks like vanishing.

When craft is the mirror (judgment, preparation, clarity, steadiness), you can lose a settlement and remain whole. You can tell the client the truth without bargaining with your worth. You can shake the mediator's hand, pack the binder, and go home without dragging the wreckage through your front door.

I think about that Wednesday more than the cases that wrapped with champagne emails. Not because it gifted me a slogan, but because it exposed the deal I'd made with myself: I'll carry the cape if you keep telling me I'm the kind of person who never drops it. When the cape didn't fly, I met the person underneath: competent, flawed, and still invited to the table tomorrow.

We love to win. Fine. Keep loving it. But let winning be a result, not a religion. Let a dead settlement be a hard fact, not a referendum on your right to belong. The need to win got many of us here. The ability to keep showing up when the other side walks is what keeps us human.

DISCOVERY REQUEST

If all the wins disappeared tomorrow, who would still remain? What would make that person enough? That's the question this Exhibit wants you to stop hiding from.

OBJECTIONS

Objection No. 1:
"But wins are what prove my value."

Overruled. Wins prove performance. They do not prove worth. Your value is shown in the consistency of your judgment, your preparation, your steadiness, and your integrity—not in the scoreboard. Wins are nice. Worth is non-negotiable.

Objection No. 2:
"But without wins, I won't be respected."

Sustained—with modification. Yes, competence earns respect. But the respect that lasts comes from character. I've seen lawyers win cases and lose the room because their ego took the victory lap. I've seen others lose a motion and gain lifelong trust because they handled it with honesty and grace. Wins get attention. Character earns loyalty.

RULING & RELIEF REQUESTED

Ruling
Success is evidence of effort, not identity. You are the lawyer, not the verdict.

Relief Requested
Complete your Worth Audit today. Separate your humanity from your highlight reel. This is the moment you renegotiate the contract between you and your worth.

SETTLEMENT TERMS

Add these to your Peace Clause Addendum in the Daily Docket for Peace:

- Achievement is temporary. Integrity is permanent.
- You are the advocate, not the outcome.
- Self-worth is non-delegable authority.

This is the doctrine of enough.

CLOSING ARGUMENT

Wins are wonderful. They validate effort, skill, and craft. But they are not you. You are the person who shows up, through complexity, through chaos, through shifting odds, with care and craft and heart. You are more than the outcomes you chase.

You are the one doing the chasing. And that, your courage, your effort, your humanity is the real victory.

COURT ORDERS

1. The Worth Audit (This Week)
Write down three wins you're proud of.

For each, *ask:*

- *Did this make me love myself more?*
- *Did it make me secure—or just distract me from insecurity?*
- *Who would I be without it?*

Then write down three losses you've carried:

- *Did they destroy me?*
- *What did I learn that I couldn't have otherwise?*
- *What part of me stayed intact in the wreckage?*

This is your evidence. This is your worth.

2. The Identity Clause (Draft & Sign This Week)
Write a short, binding clause for yourself, something you'd actually put in an agreement.

Example:
"My identity shall not merge with outcomes. Wins may be celebrated, losses may be grieved, but neither shall define the whole agreement of who I am."

Print it. Sign it. Treat it like your governing law.

3. Rewrite the Language

Whenever you feel pulled toward scoreboard thinking, replace:

"I won" with "I showed up well."
"I lost" with "I showed up."

Effort is within your control.
Identity is yours alone.
Outcome is a third party with its own agenda.

PART III

Redefining 'Enough'

PART III

Redefining Enough

Law doesn't have a finish line. Neither does ambition. Every verdict leads to another trial. Every deal leads to another demand. Every success quietly resets the standard for what "good enough" means. That's why lawyers live in a constant state of "almost there."

Almost rested. Almost satisfied. Almost free. The problem isn't that we don't achieve enough. It's that we don't allow achievement to mean anything before we move the goalpost again. This section invites you to stop running. To pause the race. To step out of closing arguments and into something quieter—and more brave. To ask the simplest, hardest question of all:

What if I'm already enough?

Because here's the truth most lawyers never argue for: there is no final verdict of success that will make you feel whole. Wholeness comes from presence, boundaries, and the courage to stop chasing "someday."

EXHIBIT ELEVEN

The Art of Enough

> *The longer I live, the more I read, the more patiently I think, and the more anxiously I inquire, the less I seem to know...Do justly. Love mercy. Walk humbly. This is enough.*
>
> —John Adams

BACKGROUND

I thought the corner office would feel like an arrival. New title, new responsibility for managing my team, my name in the board deck.

The first week in the C-suite, I stood in my office after hours, city lights stitched across the dark like a closing argument you could hang your hat on. The title, the salary, the seat, it was supposed to be the finish line. Instead, the room felt a half-size too big. My calendar didn't get lighter; it multiplied.

"Enough" stopped being about getting there and became about staying there, performing without pause. It was like climbing a mountain and finding a sign at the summit that read: NEXT PEAK, FIVE MILES UP.

If you're a lawyer, odds are you've never really believed in enough. There's always another deal to close. Another email to send. Another milestone to chase. Another vacation you "earned" but canceled for a client call. Success in law is a moving goalpost. The firm never says, "You're good now. Go be whole." Clients don't say, "You've done enough. Rest easy." The calendar doesn't stop scheduling meetings that chew your peace. So the real question is this: what does enough even look like, and would you recognize it if you already had it?

The culture whispers that fulfillment is always one step away. Once I make partner. Once I go in-house. Once I hit seven figures. Once I can finally retire. Then the cross-examination no one wants: once you get there, the feeling fades. The silence after the win feels suspicious. The stillness feels unsafe. So you do what you've been trained to do—move, chase, grind, prove. Another year disappears behind a stack of briefs and an inbox full of validation requests.

I used to mistake almost-there for a strategy. I'd "reward" myself with a night off, then fill it with email because rest without justification felt like negligence. I'd hit a goal, then immediately widen the goal until it absorbed the win. I told myself I was ambitious; sometimes I was just afraid of the quiet. Quiet might force the harder inventory: If I'm not chasing, who am I? What do I feel when the scoreboard goes dim?

Enough is not mediocrity. Enough is design. It's choosing your own metrics instead of renting them from the loudest room. It's knowing when to build and when to breathe. It's ambition with edges, purpose that knows where it stops so a life can fit around it.

Enough is a quiet rebellion in a profession that treats exhaustion like a credential. It doesn't shrink your world; it right-sizes it.

This isn't an argument against excellence. Excellence thrives inside boundaries. Without them, "more" becomes a creed you can never satisfy. More hours, more wins, more reach, more reputation. Each hit buys you fifteen minutes of relief and a fresh appetite for the same hunger. You become a connoisseur of almost: almost rested, almost satisfied, almost free.

The problem isn't that you don't achieve enough. It's that you don't let achievement mean anything before you move the post again.

When I finally looked straight at that pattern, I saw who it hurt. Teams forced to match my pace to earn my approval. Kids learning that attention must be purchased with achievement. A body trained to run on cortisol and caffeine. A self that only felt real when a scoreboard lit up. That's not drive; that is dependency.

So I started asking different questions. Not "Did I win?" but "What was the quality of my attention while I worked?" Not "Did I answer instantly?" but "Did I decide wisely?" Not "How much did I do?" but "What did I choose not to do so the important things could get my best?" The answers didn't make me smaller. They made me truer. The work didn't suffer. It got cleaner. Fewer theatrics. More judgment.

Enough looks ordinary from the outside. It looks like leaving on time without an apology.

It looks like telling a client the sober truth instead of theatrically saving the day. It looks like guarding a weekend and refusing to launder that boundary through a calendar excuse. It looks like a win that counts because you let it land before you chase the next. It looks like loss that hurts without becoming a referendum on your right to belong.

If law has no finish line, you won't find freedom by running faster. You find it by declaring the race over where it has always been over: in your own definition of a life well practiced. Wholeness doesn't come from verdicts or deals or inboxes drained. It comes from the quiet conviction that you were never on trial to begin with and from the courage to live like that's true. Enough isn't a demotion. It's permission.

It's the moment you step off the moving walkway, stand on your own feet, and realize the ground beneath you has been solid the whole time.

DISCOVERY REQUEST

What would your life look like if you finally stopped trying to win it?
Not improve it.
Not optimize it.
Not compete with it.
Just live it.

OBJECTIONS

Objection No. 1:
"But if I stop chasing, won't I fall behind?"

Overruled. Behind whom?
The LinkedIn victory parade?
Your Civil Procedure classmates from 2006?
Your own fantasy projection of who you "should" be by now?
Enough isn't comparative. It's personal jurisdiction. The only finish line that matters is the one that lets you rest in your own skin.

Objection No. 2
"If I settle for enough, won't I get lazy?"

Sustained—with modification. Complacency exists, sure.
But so does burnout. So does sleep deprivation. So does hollow "success" that costs you your life. Enough isn't giving up. Enough is ambition with intention. It's not lowering the bar; it's moving it to a sane height.

RULING & RELIEF REQUESTED

Ruling
Enough is not the absence of ambition.
It's the presence of peace.

Relief Requested
Write your personal definition of "enough" today.
Post it where you'll see it before every major decision.
This is your first act of sovereignty.

SETTLEMENT TERMS

Add these to your Daily Docket for Peace:

- Enough is not mediocrity. It is maturity.
- Chasing endlessly is not excellence; it's exhaustion in a nice suit.
- Freedom begins when you stop trying to bill your way into worthiness.

These are your terms of settlement—with yourself.

CLOSING ARGUMENT

You won't abide by your "enough" every day. You'll slip. You'll chase again. You'll get seduced by the scoreboard. We all do. But every time you return to enough, you reclaim a piece of yourself from the grind. Enough doesn't mean small. It doesn't mean lazy. It doesn't mean settling. It means free. And freedom, last I checked, is worth more than any billable hour.

COURT ORDERS

1. Define Your Enough (This Week)
Draft your definition.

Ask yourself:

- *What does "enough" look like for me—in work, money, relationships, health?*

- *If I stopped chasing, what would I have space for?*

- *What am I doing just to look successful, not to feel fulfilled?*

Then write one sentence that defines your enough. Examples: '*Enough*' *means…*

- *I can leave the office at six and still sleep at night.*
- *paying the bills without sacrificing every weekend.*
- *being courtside for the game, not on my phone.*

Print it. Post it. Live by it, not as a finish line, but as a compass.

2. The Enough Inventory (By Week's End)
List 10 things you already have that once felt impossible:

- Jobs.
- Relationships.
- Health.
- Milestones.
- Moments.

Sit with the list. Notice how fast each "arrival" faded into the background.

Then ask:
What if these were enough right now?

Let gratitude become a metric, not an afterthought.

3. Add a New Clause to Your Peace Contract

Write this down:
"I am allowed to rest before I am finished."

Not after the hundredth task.
Not after inbox zero.
Not after winning whatever imaginary contest you're running in your head. *Before*.

Rest is not a luxury. It's maintenance.

EXHIBIT TWELVE

Presence Over Perfection

> *The best is the enemy of the good.*
>
> —Voltaire
>
> *who would have gone in-house to avoid billable hours.

BACKGROUND

My Zoom calls from my home office had ended late again, my brain buzzing and my stomach empty. I stood up and walked into the kitchen. My daughter met me with a grin and a piece of paper clutched in both hands.

"I made you something." I crouched, phone still warm in my palm, and said the line I've mastered:

"That's amazing, honey."

I kissed her head, grabbed a glass of water, and drifted back into my home office when my phone vibrated.

An hour later, I found the drawing on the floor of my office, abandoned with the kind of quiet only kids can manage. I picked it up. It was a wild galaxy of markers: a lopsided tree house with our stick-figure family holding hands on the largest branch. I realized I hadn't actually seen it. Not really. I'd performed presence while my brain kept litigating the day. She knew it. And that stung more than any courtroom loss I've ever had.

Perfection always demands distance. Distance from the moment. Distance from the people around you. Distance from yourself.

When you're perfect, you're managing, curating, performing. When you're present, you're just there. No script. No polish. No mental closing arguments. And being "just there" is a skill most lawyers have long since unlearned.

Picture it:

- a one-on-one with a team member.
- A hard conversation with your partner.
- Your kid telling a chaotic story about Minecraft, pillow forts, or a YouTuber you've never heard of.

You want to be there. But the ticker starts rolling:

- *Did I forget to reply to that email?*
- *Did I sound stupid in that meeting?*
- *I should've said it differently.*
- *I need to circle back on that deck.*
- *Am I doing enough?*

So, you nod. You smile. You "mm-hmm" at all the right times. But you're not in the moment; you're managing it from a mental control tower that's rerunning today, previewing tomorrow, and editing a transcript no one else can see. That's the cost of perfection: it robs you of presence, then convinces you no one noticed.

The profession trains this into us. Law is a performance art dressed as analysis. You rehearse. You polish. You anticipate counterarguments and risks and optics.

It works in court. It wins in conference rooms. But transplant that same reflex into a kitchen or a 1:1 and you get a person who looks engaged while, in truth, is running a silent appeal. You become a museum guard for your own life, near the art, never with it.

Perfection whispers that presence is risky. If you stop managing, you might miss something. If you stop curating, someone might see a rough edge. If you stop performing, they might decide you're ordinary. So you stage-manage dinner, strategize bedtime, treat a colleague's vulnerability like a problem set. You leave the conversation having "handled it," but nothing actually touched you. And the people you love learn a quiet math: to get your attention, they must bring a crisis or a trophy.

That night with the drawing, I recognized the trial I'd been running without a judge: the invisible case called Prove You're Still Worthy. Every ping was evidence. Every pause was negligence. I wasn't ignoring my daughter out of neglect; I was ignoring her out of perfectionism—still fighting the day's phantom jurors to keep from getting something "wrong" at work, even if it meant getting it wrong at home.

Presence is not passivity. It's consent to reality. It's the choice to inhabit the exact square foot of life you are standing in, unarmored. It's letting a teammate finish their thought without drafting your rebuttal. It's holding your partner's eyes when the conversation turns sharp. It's kneeling at 8:47 p.m. to truly look at a marker-made tree house and asking, "Tell me about this incredible tree house." It's trusting that your competence doesn't evaporate if you stop narrating it for five minutes.

Perfection keeps you safe from embarrassment; presence keeps you close to what matters. Perfection optimizes optics; presence deepens contact. Perfection makes you admirable; presence makes you available. One builds a résumé. The other builds a life. If law has taught me anything useful here, it's that facts beat performance. The facts were simple: a child drew a tree house and offered me room in it; I declined for a notification. That's not a scheduling issue. That's a misalignment of values camouflaged as diligence.

I folded that drawing up and put it in my desk drawer. Not as penance, though it humbled me, but as a witness.

A map back to the only place law can't teach you to stand: here. Not drafting, not defending, not predicting. Just here. The emails still arrive. The meetings still multiply. The part of me that loves a clean argument still warms up in the bullpen. But the distance that perfection demands doesn't get the final word as often. Presence isn't tidy. It doesn't clap for you. It just holds the moment long enough for you to feel it. And that, quietly and stubbornly, is where enough begins.

DISCOVERY REQUEST

When was the last time you felt fully present, and what made it possible? Let that memory be your baseline. Presence is often something you've already tasted—just not protected.

OBJECTIONS

Objection No. 1
"But if I let go of polish, I'll look unprofessional."

Overruled. Your kids don't need polish. Your partner doesn't want polish. Your friends don't crave polish. They crave you, the unedited, unstacked, non-performative version. Even clients know the difference between someone being in the room and someone performing for it. Presence builds trust faster than polish ever has.

Objection No. 2
"But presence feels inefficient."

Sustained—with clarification. Presence is slower. It wanders. It doesn't fit neatly into six-minute increments. But inefficiency isn't waste, it's texture. You don't remember the efficient interactions. You remember the moments where you were actually with someone. Presence looks unproductive on paper. It produces the only things that matter off of it.

RULING & RELIEF REQUESTED

Ruling

Perfectionism is performance. Presence is power.

Relief Requested

Choose one interaction today: with a child, partner, friend, or colleague, and meet it with total, undivided presence. No rehearsal. No fixing. No phone. No polish. Just you.

SETTLEMENT TERMS

Add these to your Daily Docket for Peace:

- Presence outperforms perfection in every human context.
- Efficiency builds careers; attention builds lives.
- Your presence is not a productivity metric, it is a gift.

These are the non-negotiable
terms of a connected life.

CLOSING ARGUMENT

Presence isn't a permanent state; it's a choice you return to often, imperfectly. You'll drift. You'll forget. You'll rehearse conversations in your head instead of living the one in front of you. But every time you come back, even for a few seconds, the room softens. The people you love feel it. And so do you.

Perfection wants applause.
Presence wants honesty.

Only one of them builds a life worth practicing. The people who love you don't want the polished version of you. They want the real one. The one who kneels down at 8:47 p.m. and says,
"Tell me about this incredible tree house."

COURT ORDERS

1. The Imperfect Attention Practice
Once this week, give someone your full attention, completely and consciously.

- No multitasking.
- No "thinking ahead."
- No silent rebuttals or analysis.

Just be in the same moment, at the same pace, on the same planet. It will feel vulnerable. That's the point.

2. The Three-Minute Drill
Set a timer for three minutes while someone you care about talks.
Your job:

- Don't interrupt.
- Don't advise.
- Don't redirect.
- Don't perform.

Your mind will twitch. Let it. This is the workout.

3. Add This Clause to Your Peace Contract

Write and post:

"I will not confuse performing with connecting."

Your one-sentence line item to break the spell of perfection when it creeps back in.

EXHIBIT THIRTEEN

Rewriting the Narrative

> *The future has several names. For the weak, it is impossible. For the fainthearted, it is unknown. For the thoughtful and valiant, it is ideal.*
>
> —Victor Hugo

BACKGROUND

I walked out of a board meeting and immediately started cross-examining myself. In my head, the story wrote itself fast and clean:

They think I'm not strategic enough.
They saw through me. I'm the kid from law
school who lucked into the room.

I replayed every sentence I'd uttered, searching for the line that "proved" it. The hallway got longer. The elevator felt like a verdict chamber. Then someone from the board meeting caught the door and stepped in beside me.

"Good session," she said, scrolling her phone.

"The legal evolution overview helped a ton."

The doors slid shut. No theater. No eyebrow raises. Just a normal exit from a normal meeting. The story in my head swallowed its cape and pretended it hadn't been performing for the last ten minutes.

Every lawyer I know is good at storytelling, for other people. We help clients frame their cases. We draft narratives that persuade, anticipate rebuttals, and tie it up with a closing that leaves no doubt who's right. But when it comes to our own lives, we're often stuck in the wrong story. Worse, we don't realize it. We write a tight plot about who we are and how the world sees us, then treat it like binding precedent. You may not say it out loud, but there's a running script in your head. It sounds like this:

- *I must be the one who fixes this.*
- *If I don't hold it all together, everything falls apart.*
- *I'm only valuable when I'm performing.*
- *I can't rest until it's all perfect.*
- *If I let go, they'll see I'm not enough.*

That script becomes your identity. Default operating system. Inner jurisprudence. And here's the kicker: most of it was written by fear. Not the truth. Not values. Not who you want to be. Just fear dressed in a suit, carrying a briefcase, whispering in your ear with perfect diction.

Fear-craft is convincing because it uses our tools. It cites out-of-context facts: *remember that one time you stumbled?*

Mis-states holdings: *one critique means you're incompetent.* And files emergency motions in your nervous system.

It's also lazy with evidence. The record against you is mostly feeling; the counter-record: praise, trust, repeated invitations back into the room, gets excluded as "irrelevant."

The result is a narrative you'd dismantle in five minutes if a client brought it to you, but which you carry like a notarized truth when it's yours.

That board meeting was textbook. My internal brief read: *they think I'm not strategic; I don't belong.* The actual record: no one blinked; they thanked me; they moved on.

I had authored a drama of inadequacy and cast everyone else as bit players without a shred of support. We are dangerous authors when we never question our own drafts.

The stories we live inside show up everywhere once you start noticing them. The partner's curt email becomes a chapter titled "I'm Failing."

A client's silence becomes they've lost confidence in me. A teammate's independent win becomes I'm being replaced.

None of these are facts; they're interpretations dressed as facts, stapled to your ribs by an old belief about worth. The belief predates the job—family systems, early school, the first time excellence earned you love. Law just gave you vocabulary and a profession.

There's another move fear makes. It turns roles into destinies. "Fixer" becomes savior. "High standards" becomes impossible standards. "Responsive" becomes on-call. Pretty soon, the narrator in your head speaks in inevitable language: I must, I always, I can't. That's not a memoir; that's a sentence.

Meanwhile, in the external world, life keeps offering you conflicting evidence: colleagues who lean on you because they trust you, not because you never err; leaders who absorb setbacks and still want you in the next room; people outside of work who couldn't care less about your highlight reel and just want you at dinner, eyes up. The mind trained for litigation treats these as exceptions. But exceptions, piled high enough, are just the rule you've been ignoring. What would it read like to author from values instead of fear? The voice changes.

Fear says: *If I don't hold this together, everything falls apart.*

Values say: *I'm a steward, not a savior.*

Fear says: *I'm only valuable when I'm performing.*

Values say: *My presence is part of the value.*

Fear says: *I can't rest until it's perfect.*
Values say: *Excellence is accuracy, clarity, ethics, and enough sleep to do them again.*

Notice how the plot loosens when the narrator tells the truth. This isn't about self-help slogans. It's about narrative fidelity. As lawyers, we respect the record. We separate allegations from proof. We know when a witness is testifying beyond personal knowledge.

Apply that to your own story and whole scenes collapse: the imagined panel of judges in your head disbands; the jury of past critics goes home; the opposing counsel named Everyone's Opinion loses standing. What remains is smaller and saner: people, work, meaning, fallibility, yours and theirs. The story you choose shapes the life you live.

If the script is:
"*I'm only safe when I'm winning,*"
you'll engineer a life of ceaseless trial.

If the script is:
"*I earn belonging by being indispensable,*"
you'll design relationships where rest equals exile.

If the script is:
"*I'm allowed to be human here,*" rooms open. Options multiply.
The nervous system lowers its shoulders.

When I think back to the elevator ride following the board meeting, what stands out now isn't the offhand compliment; it's the realization that my mind had been staging a play in an empty theater.

I had written a closing argument for a case no one was hearing. I was both the only audience and the only juror. That's the quiet absurdity of so many lawyer stories we tell ourselves: meticulously constructed, ferociously argued, entirely untried.

We don't have to throw away the craft to change the story. Keep the discipline. Keep the clarity. Keep the love of a well-placed fact. But let the narrator be someone you'd trust with your own client: curious, proportionate, anchored in evidence, accountable to values. Fear can file its briefs; it just doesn't get the last word.

DISCOVERY REQUEST

What self-invented narrative about yourself have you been treating as sworn testimony, and what would happen if you struck it from the record? Sit with it. Let it sting a little. That sting is truth waking up.

OBJECTIONS

Objection No. 1
"But my story has always been this way."

Overruled. In court, precedent binds. In life, it doesn't. Just because you've lived one version of yourself doesn't mean you're bound to it. Stories change when authors grow, and you're allowed to grow.

- You can unsettle your own case law.
- You can vacate old judgments.
- You can overturn narratives that never should've survived appeal.

Objection No. 2:
"Rewriting the story feels fake."
Sustained—with context.

Yes, rewriting feels unnatural. So did practicing law the first year. So did leadership. So did vulnerability.

Rewriting your internal story isn't lying. It's editing. It's authorship.

It's choosing to tell the truth instead of the loudest fear.

If your old story was written by panic, why not let your updated story be written by experience, compassion, and actual evidence?

RULING & RELIEF REQUESTED

Ruling
The narrative you live by is not binding precedent. You may amend at any time, without leave of court.

Relief Requested
Write your new opening statement today, and read it aloud before your next major decision. Let it set the tone. Let it re-center the narrator.

SETTLEMENT TERMS

Add the following to your governing law:

- Familiarity does not equal truth.
- Self-awareness is not weakness, it is cross-examination.
- You are not the evidence. You are the author.
- Fear may advise, but it may not decide.

CLOSING ARGUMENT

This isn't a one-time rewrite. It's an ongoing editorial process. Some days the old script will win, fine. You're human. But the more you return to authorship, the more your life starts sounding like you again. You weren't built to live inside a story written by fear. You were built to write the kind of story you'd be proud to inhabit.

You were never the narrative.
You were always the narrator.

COURT ORDERS

1. Draft a New Opening Statement

Start with:
"I'm learning to..."
"I'm no longer willing to..."
"I believe in..."
"I forgive myself for..."
"I'm becoming the kind of lawyer who..."

It does not need to be polished. It needs to be true.

2. Cross-Examine the Old Script
Pick one negative narrative, like:
"I'm not enough."
"I'm always one mistake away from being exposed."
"If I slow down, everything falls apart."

Now: Present your evidence.
Identify unreliable witnesses: *fear, shame, comparison.* Call your wiser self to the stand.

Issue findings:
What is true?
What is dismissed with prejudice?

Treat your story like testimony, not gospel.

3. Add to Your Peace Contract
Write and post:
"I am not on trial for who I used to be."

Tape it somewhere you can't avoid it.

EXHIBIT FOURTEEN

Letting Go, Everyday

> *To let go does not mean to get rid of. To let go means to let be. When we let be with compassion, things come and go on their own.*
>
> —Jack Kornfield

BACKGROUND

It didn't happen on a beach. It happened on a Friday that looked like every other Friday, gray sky and clouds, a mental to-do list a mile long, and an inbox already overflowing. I decided to run an experiment: no grand gestures, just small releases. I let a curt email sit. I ignored a typo no one else would notice. I closed my laptop at 4:30 p.m. because I'd said I would.

That night, my youngest daughter looked at me and said,

"You seem happy."

She didn't know why, but she felt it. That's when it clicked: letting go wasn't a cinematic quit. It was maintenance. Repetition. A daily pattern of release that changes the weather inside your own chest.

Here's the thing no one tells you: letting go isn't a one-time event. There's no slow-motion scene where you drop your briefcase in the sand, stare at the ocean, and feel free forever.

Letting go is a discipline that keeps you from confusing tightness with control. Every morning, you wake up with two choices: clench or breathe. Most lawyers choose clench. It's the reflex. You grab your phone before your glasses. You check your inbox before your pulse.

You feel behind before your feet touch the ground. But that isn't a law of physics; it's a habit. You can choose a different rhythm. You don't have to be perfect at it. You just have to practice.

We're trained for the opposite. Law rewards grip: anticipate, contain, outwork. Useful in a record; ruinous as a lifestyle.

The muscles we strengthen at work (control, critique, contingency) can calcify everything else. You start narrating your life like a closing argument: explain, justify, preempt. Letting go is the counter-muscle. Not apathy, not surrender: just the refusal to make every moment a referendum on your competence. On an average Tuesday, it looks like very small things add up:

- *Choosing no response or email until you've had coffee.*
- *Not spiraling over a partner's vague tone.*
- *Saying "I don't know" without shame.*
- *Leaving when you said you would.*
- *Asking for help before you break.*
- *Letting the meeting be awkward.*
- *Not fixing your kid's problem immediately.*
- *Breathing before reacting.*
- *Letting silence be enough.*
- *Closing your laptop even when there's more to do.*
- *Laughing when something goes sideways.*
- *Forgiving yourself for the thing you're still mad about.*
- *Saying no without a 600-word apology.*

None of these moments are dramatic. But string them together, and your nervous system starts getting the message: we're allowed to be human here. The day stops feeling like a cross-examination you must ace. The room gets quieter, and not because the world calmed down, but because you did.

Letting go also rewrites the story you tell about your worth. Clench says, "If I don't hold it all together, everything falls apart." Breathe says, "I'm a steward, not a savior." Clench says, "I'm only valuable when I'm performing." Breathe says, "Presence is part of the value."

Clench makes every ping an alarm. Breathe turns alarms back into information. Same facts, different posture.

There's nothing glamorous about practice. You won't get an all-firm email for choosing not to react to a 10:02 a.m. nudge at 10:07 a.m. No one hands you a trophy for letting your kid finish a tangled story without turning it into a life lesson. But these are the reps that move the needle where it matters most: the quality of your attention, the steadiness of your teams, the way your people relax around you because you're not auditioning for invincibility anymore.

That Friday experiment taught me something embarrassingly simple: happiness didn't arrive; noise left. Not all at once, not permanently, but just enough to notice. The world didn't reward me for loosening my grip; it didn't punish me either. The client still called. The work still existed. Only now, the person doing it wasn't running an invisible trial called Prove You're Still Worthy. He was just working, clearer, kinder, and more here.

Letting go won't make your life tidy. It will make it livable. Tomorrow morning, the fork will still be there: clench or breathe. You'll choose a dozen times before lunch. Some you'll miss. That's fine. This isn't a verdict. It's a practice. A way of coming home to yourself, over and over again, until one ordinary night, someone who loves you says, "You seem happy," and you realize they're right.

DISCOVERY REQUEST

What's one thing you could let go of today that would make tomorrow lighter? Make it small. Make it human. Make it honest. It could be the offhand comment that's still riding shotgun in your mind. The mistake you keep replaying like it's breaking news. The tension in your shoulders that arrived at 8:17 a.m. and never left. Pick something real, something your body would thank you for releasing. Let it go the way you put down a heavy grocery bag: not ceremoniously, just because you're tired of carrying it.

OBJECTIONS

Objection No. 1:
"But it feels pointless if I have to keep doing it."

Overruled.
You eat every day.
You breathe every day.
You sleep every day.

Maintenance isn't proof of failure, it's proof of wisdom. It means you understand that peace isn't a destination, it's upkeep. Repeating the practice doesn't mean it's not working. It just means you're human, with a nervous system that needs reminders, not miracles. Letting go over and over again isn't regression, it's rhythm.

Objection No. 2
"I barely have time for what's already on my plate."

Sustained—with modification. Your schedule is tight. Your calendar is a game of Tetris with no clean lines. But letting go isn't a meeting. It's a posture you bring into every meeting. It's the difference between gripping your briefcase with white-knuckled urgency or carrying it like someone who trusts their own strength and doesn't fear the next step. Time isn't the bottleneck. Awareness is the unlock. A one-breath shift can change the entire hour that follows.

RULING & RELIEF REQUESTED

Ruling
Letting go is not a one-time epiphany you frame on your wall. It's a daily discipline, quiet, stubborn, and protective, that guards your peace as fiercely as it guards your practice.

Motion for Immediate Relief
Tomorrow morning, choose one Daily Dismissal. Write it down. Say it out loud. Cross it out like it owes you money. Small. Simple. Real. But watch how the smallest release cracks open the day.

SETTLEMENT TERMS

- Letting go is not weakness; it's intelligence sharpened by experience.
- Freedom isn't granted once it's renewed through daily choices.
- Your worth isn't determined by what you cling to; it's revealed by what you're willing to release.
- Slow, steady practice beats dramatic reinvention. Every. Single. Time.

CLOSING ARGUMENT

This book isn't about abandoning ambition. It's about returning to yourself, the part that existed before the accolades and the anxiety.

- *Letting go is not collapse. It's calibration.*
- *A reset, reprioritization or remembering.*
- *You can be brilliant without being brittle.*
- *You can lead without losing yourself.*
- *You can succeed without suffocating.*

Letting go isn't the opposite of lawyering, it's what makes the rest of your life possible. You still get to be a damn good lawyer. You just don't have to be a clenched one.

COURT ORDERS

1. Keep a Daily Dismissal List
For the next seven days, write down one item each morning:

- a fear that insists on narrating over your confidence
- a responsibility that was never yours but somehow landed on your desk
- a mistake you're still prosecuting long after everyone else moved on
- a mood someone else handed you that you didn't actually want
- a worry about tomorrow that doesn't belong to today

Write one clear sentence, then cross it out like a judge who's done deliberating.

2. The Evening Check-In
Before bed, *ask yourself:*
Where did I cling today?
Where did I let go?

Celebrate the releases, even the tiny ones.

Forgive the gripping: your humanity was showing. Then close the case for the day, mentally setting the file back on the shelf.

3. Add to Your Peace Contract

Write and post:
"I am allowed to rest before I am finished."

This clause stays.
No amendments. No footnotes. No exceptions.

PART IV

Beyond the Illusions

PART IV

Beyond the Illusions

This final section examines the illusions that keep us sprinting long after we're spent:

- the promise of someday
- the tyranny of urgency
- the weight of comparison
- the fantasy of balance and
- the addiction of achievement.

These are the myths that whisper: *keep going, just a little more, one last thing.* They disguise themselves as drive, ambition, professionalism. But beneath it all, they're fear in a tailored suit.

- Fear of slowing down.
- Fear of being ordinary.
- Fear of being still.

Part IV asks you to challenge those illusions one by one. To question the "*someday*" you've been building your life around. To interrogate the constant urgency you mistake for importance.

To cross-examine comparison, balance, and success—and see what's left when the illusions rest their case. This isn't about giving up. It's about giving yourself back. Because the truth is simple: peace isn't earned through exhaustion. It's claimed through surrender.

EXHIBIT FIFTEEN

The Myth of Someday

> *Life is what happens when you are busy making other plans.*
>
> —John Lennon
>
> *Would've despised time sheets.

BACKGROUND

It was a weeknight in a hotel in some city I cannot remember, away from home for another trial, rain bouncing off the hotel room window while I told myself the same thing I had been telling myself for years: *After this trial ends, things will calm down. Then I can get back to living.* But I had been reaching for that invisible day for years and I was no closer in that moment than I had been before.

Lawyers are fluent in Someday. We tell ourselves: *When the trial is over, I'll rest. When the deal closes, I'll take that trip. When I make partner, I'll finally feel like enough.* But here's the thing about Someday: it never arrives.

As soon as one deadline passes, another appears. As soon as you crest one mountain, another waits: same slope, new scenery, identical exhaustion. Someday is a moving target that keeps you hustling through your present life like it's a layover on the way to your real one.

I used to pitch "just for now" like a strategy. After this quarter. After this filing. After this month-long trial in another city. After we get through diligence. My family could finish the sentence for me; they knew the cadence. What I called temporary, they experienced as normal. That's how deferred life syndrome works: you keep promising a calmer future while training everyone you love to live without you today. We tell ourselves sacrifice is temporary, that we're stockpiling peace and joy for later. But unlike billable hours, those don't accrue. You can't bank missed birthdays, unused vacation days, or quiet mornings with your kids. Once they're gone, they're gone.

Someday is seductive because it sounds responsible. It isn't procrastination; it's planning. It isn't avoidance; it's discipline. You imagine a future where the inbox is tame, the team is staffed, the partner is reasonable, the judge is on schedule, the market is stable, and you finally are allowed to exhale. But the profession is designed to refill the plate you just cleared. Trials move; deals revive; clients pivot; leadership changes the objective; your own ambition resets the bar. The treadmill's speed button is always closer than the stop key.

And the body keeps the receipts. You learn to run on adrenaline, caffeine, and the belief that you're one heroic push from freedom.

You become excellent at sprinting and terrible at arriving. Even when a window opens (a case settles, a trial date is continued, a light docket presents itself), you feel itchy. Stillness reads as risk. Silence sounds like failure. So you do what you've trained to do: move. Chase. Prove. "Rest" turns into organizing the garage while checking email. "Vacation" becomes a different desk with worse Wi-Fi.

The harm isn't only personal. Someday thinking bleeds into teams. You tell juniors the crush is temporary while staffing them into the next crush. You defer hard conversations because "it's crazy right now," only to discover that crazy is your baseline. You promise clients velocity instead of truth because you don't want to admit the timeline is fiction. The bill comes due in burnout, brittle culture, and work that's efficient instead of wise.

The cruel part is that Someday occasionally pays out: just enough to keep the story alive. A case ends early. A negotiation closes. You get a weekend that feels like oxygen. You start to believe the system can be hacked. Then the calendar tugs your sleeve, and the next "last push" steps up like a polite assassin. It isn't a conspiracy; it's physics. Work expands to the size of your life if you let it.

What does "enough" time look like if Someday never shows? It looks like deciding that the present isn't a lobby. It looks like refusing to mortgage today's ordinary moments for a hypothetical future that never signs the closing documents. It looks like building a life that can be lived during, not after.

I remember the first time I said no to a 'quick Sunday touch-base.' It was a random afternoon, nothing special. We were in the backyard, and my son was trying to bank a whiffle ball off the fence into the pool. He missed twenty times, laughing harder with each failure like he'd discovered a loophole in physics.

My phone buzzed; the subject line had the usual urgency dressings. I looked at him, at the pool, at the sky that wasn't recording any of this for later, and I chose to miss the call. No fireworks. No moral victory montage. Just a quiet refusal to donate another slice of a finite day to the myth of later. I took off my Apple watch and put my phone on the charger. I was deliberate about drawing a line, and, at least in that moment, trading Someday for today.

Someday tells you that life will settle once you've earned it. Life doesn't settle. It flows. Some stretches are whitewater; some are glass. You don't get to hold the river still. You get a boat, a paddle, and the right to choose how much of the ride you'll inhabit. If you're waiting for the perfect patch of calm before you show up (at home, with friends, for yourself), you'll miss the river for the map.

I still catch myself bargaining with tomorrow. In busy seasons, the old line tries to sneak back: *after this filing... after this quarter ends... after this one more thing.* Sometimes I believe it. More often, I hear the click in my own voice and stop mid-sentence. Not because work isn't important, but because "later" isn't where my life lives. The only place it ever has is here: Thursday dinner out, messy kitchen, lopsided shot into a bucket, a phone face-down while a story about Minecraft and Roblox and some YouTuber unspools without a closing argument.

Someday was never going to save me. It was just going to keep me running. I don't want a life that begins after the sprint. I want the kind that lets me breathe during the marathon.

DISCOVERY REQUEST

What "*Someday*" dream has been waiting on your signature, and what happens if you execute it now? Let it be specific. Let it be embarrassingly ordinary. Not "write the great American novel," more like:

- Eat breakfast without my phone.
- Call my brother back.
- Take a walk that isn't multitasking.
- Read ten pages of the book I bought two years ago.
- Plan a weekend that isn't a pit stop.

Someday is just Today with better branding. Name the thing you keep postponing, and tell the truth about why.

OBJECTIONS

Objection No. 1
"But I have to sacrifice now to build security later."

Sustained—in part. Yes, seasons of grind exist. Yes, you're building something real. But if every season becomes a sacrifice, then sacrifice isn't a season, it's your personality. Security built on self-erasure won't feel secure when you finally get there. You can invest in your future without repossessing your present.

Objection No. 2
"Things will calm down after this case/quarter/deal."

Overruled. You've told yourself this a hundred times. On good days, you even believe it. But the profession isn't designed for equilibrium. It is engineered for escalation. The calm you're idolizing isn't scheduled, it's something you must claim.

And here's the secret: You don't need the world to slow down. You just need to stop sprinting past your own life.

RULING & RELIEF REQUESTED

Ruling
Someday is not a strategy. Someday is a stall tactic dressed up as ambition. It is hereby dismissed with prejudice.

Motion for Immediate Relief
Choose one deferred joy, something real, something yours. Put it on this week's calendar. Not "when things settle." Now. Even one reclaimed moment is enough to break the spell.

SETTLEMENT TERMS

- Someday is a mirage designed to keep you compliant.
- Time is not found; it is claimed.
- Rest is not something you earn, it's something you practice.
- A life deferred becomes a life diluted.
- Today is not a rehearsal. It's the whole show.

CLOSING ARGUMENT

Stop treating your life like the closing argument you'll get to once the court clears. There is no Someday docket. There is only today's calendar and how bravely you inhabit it.

You don't need to blow up your career.
You don't need to move to a cabin.
You don't need to win the mythical "future calm."

You just need to stop outsourcing your joy to a date that never arrives. Start small. Start messy. Start now. Trade one *Someday* for one *Today*, and watch the whole architecture of your life start shifting back into the present tense.

COURT ORDERS

1. The Someday Inventory
By Friday, list five things you've been deferring:

- a trip
- a conversation
- a hobby
- a ritual
- a moment of rest you keep rescheduling

Circle one. Start it this week. Not perfectly. Not dramatically. Just begin. Momentum is built, not granted.

2. The Micro-Someday
Pick one dream you've shelved:

Someday I'll write a book.
Write one messy paragraph today.

Someday I'll get healthy.
Walk ten minutes before work.

Someday I'll reconnect with my friend.
Send a two-sentence text.

Someday I'll take that trip.
Look up a date. Put a hold on a hotel room.

You're not completing the dream. You're puncturing the illusion that life must wait until your docket clears.

3. Add to Your Peace Contract
Write this where you can see it:

"I will not defer what makes me come alive."

This clause is not negotiable. No extensions. No continuances. No Someday exceptions.

EXHIBIT SIXTEEN

The Tyranny of Urgency

> *Your lack of preparation is not my emergency.*
>
> —Lawyers
>
> *Everywhere.

BACKGROUND

The first time I realized urgency had colonized my nervous system, it was 11:04 p.m. and my phone lit up with a subject line dressed in sirens: NEED THIS BY MORNING.

I was already asleep in bed. I snapped upright, ran to grab my laptop, opened a blank doc, and sprinted (citations, framing, three options, risks color-coded) until birds started auditioning outside the window. At 8:11 a.m., I dropped the draft into the partner's email inbox and went to rinse the caffeine off my teeth. Two days later, I sat in his office and could see my "emergency" exactly where I'd left it. Unopened. The only thing that had been on fire was me.

Lawyers live under the tyranny of urgency. Every email wears a red exclamation mark.

Every client insists their matter is time-sensitive. Every partner wants it done “yesterday.” We confuse urgency with importance. We start to believe speed equals value, that responsiveness equals competence, that living in a sprint means we’re indispensable. But the tyranny of urgency carries a hidden cost: it hijacks your peace, distorts your priorities, and convinces you that everything is on fire all the time.

Life in the fire drill looks impressive from the outside. The calendar is packed, the Slack lights up, the inbox reproduces like sea monkeys. You answer in minutes, you “jump on,” you “circle back,” you live on the front foot. People thank you for being “on it,” and the dopamine does what dopamine does. The problem is what it does to judgment. When everything is urgent, nothing is weighted.

You start building arguments at the speed of adrenaline, mistaking velocity for thought. You over-communicate when silence would steady the room. You draft at 1:17 a.m. what should have waited for daylight and a brain.

I once worked for a partner who treated every request like a four-alarm blaze. Midnight emails. *“Need this by morning.”* I’d scramble, bleary-eyed, to deliver, only to find the draft untouched days later. The lesson landed in phases.

- **Phase 1:** not everything urgent is important.
- **Phase 2:** some “fires” are smoke machines—performances meant to keep us running, signals meant to reaffirm status, rehearsals for a culture that worships motion.
- **Phase 3:** the one that took too long: the real danger is when you internalize that pace, when your body learns to twitch at every ping, and you can no longer tell the difference between a true emergency and someone else’s poor planning.

Urgency also flatters the ego. It says, you are needed right now. It frames your availability as virtue and your boundaries as betrayal. It turns responsiveness into a morality play: reply in five minutes and you're a hero; reply in five hours and you're suspect. The profession's worst habits feed it: time zones ignored, "quick thoughts?" that aren't, reviews requested at 10:58 p.m. for 7:00 a.m. meetings that could have been moved. Soon, your nervous system is a smoke detector with a dying battery, beeping at everything, useful to no one.

There's a quieter cost, too. Urgency steals presence. You sit in a 1:1 and half-listen, eyes flicking to the corner of your screen. You attend your kid's game and live in the haptic ghost of a future ping. You fall asleep drafting replies in your head to emails that don't exist yet. It's not that you don't care about people; it's that the fire drill trains you to treat every moment as antechamber to the next alert. Life becomes a series of pauses between alarms.

The culture won't fix this for you. Clients will keep labeling everything as high importance. Partners will keep testing who salutes the fastest. Systems optimize for throughput, not wisdom. And because urgency occasionally aligns with reality (real crises do happen), the lie stays sticky. See? your brain says. This time it was an emergency.

So you rebuild the bunker. You set your life on "always available" because one night a year actually warrants it. That's how habits calcify: a few true fires justify a thousand drills.

What finally broke the spell for me wasn't a productivity hack; it was embarrassment. I caught myself drafting a "quick take" on my phone in an elevator while a client was mid-sentence about his father's surgery. I nodded at the wrong point, and he paused, noticing the distance. That's urgency's tell: it makes you look busy and feel important while quietly making you worse at the thing you're paid for (judgment) and the things that make you worth keeping (attention, steadiness, proportion).

None of this argues for slowness as a virtue. There are filings that cannot slip, crises that require a sprint, moments when speed is mercy. The point is discrimination. Without it, you let the loudest clock set your life. You spend brilliance on triage that didn't need it. You train teams to chase heat instead of substance. You reward the colleague who shouts "fire!" over the one who builds systems that prevent it. And you end most days with the hollow certainty that you moved a lot without moving the thing that mattered.

I still get the 11:04 p.m. emails. Some nights, they deserve the sprint. Most nights, they don't. The difference isn't in the subject line; it's in the posture I bring to it. Urgency wants to make every moment immediate. Importance asks for scale: What is this, really? What carries weight? What can wait? When I honor that hierarchy, the work improves, and the room calms. What's strange is how little the outside world notices the change. Deliverables still land. Clients still feel held. Only now, the person delivering isn't pretending to live in a permanent siren.

The fire drill is persuasive because it feels like proof of value. Let it be evidence of humanity instead: yours, theirs, everyone's messy timing. Then give the job what it truly needs: a clear head, a steady hand, and the nerve to let some smoke dissipate before you pull the alarm.

DISCOVERY REQUEST

What percentage of your stress comes from genuine urgency, and what percentage comes from reflex?

Don't brief it. Feel it.

- *How much of your week is driven by actual deadlines—filings, court dates, real risk?*
- *How much is driven by "quick thoughts?" "Circling back,"* or *"ASAP"* from people who confuse speed with substance?
- *How often do you feel your stomach drop at a subject line, and then find out it could've waited a day?*

Name the difference between real fires and smoke machines. That gap is where your peace lives.

OBJECTIONS

Objection No. 1
"But clients expect urgency."

Sustained—with limitations. Yes, clients value responsiveness. No, that does not require you to live on a hair trigger.

Clients actually want: steady judgment, clear thinking, work that holds up after the adrenaline wears off. You can't deliver that if you treat every ping like a TRO. Urgency without discernment isn't service. It's chaos in a suit.

Objection No. 2
"If I don't treat everything as urgent, I'll fall behind."

Overruled. You can be the fastest responder in the room and still be the most exhausted, least strategic person at the table.

Ask yourself:

- *Did replying at 11:07 p.m. instead of 7:07 a.m. ever truly change the outcome?*
- *Or did it just change your sleep?*

The lawyers who last aren't the ones who run the hardest. They're the ones who know when not to run.

A Quick Case Study

For years, I wore "fastest responder" like a badge. Partners loved it. My inbox did not.

One night, my phone buzzed and I sighed, loudly. My son looked up and asked, "Why do you always breathe like that when your phone rings?"

Not snarky. Just honest. That was the cross-examination I needed. Urgency wasn't just in my calendar. It had moved into my body.

RULING & RELIEF REQUESTED

Ruling

Urgency is admissible as a temporary motivator. It is inadmissible as a lifestyle.

Treating everything as a fire is hereby found to be:

- prejudicial to your judgment,
- harmful to your health, and
- contrary to the interests of justice in your actual life.

Motion for Relief Requested

This week, conduct an Urgency Audit. Notice every time something feels urgent. At day's end, mark which were truly critical, and which were just loud. Small step, big reveal. You can't reclaim your peace from a pattern you refuse to see.

SETTLEMENT TERMS

- Not all urgency is real. A lot of it is just other people's anxiety with a subject line.
- Speed is not the same as value. A rushed "yes" can be far more damaging than a measured "no."
- Slowing down is not neglect; it is professional judgment.
- Your nervous system is not a shared firm resource. It is not up for unlimited use.
- You are allowed to respond thoughtfully instead of instantly —even in law.

Tape this to your Daily Docket for Peace if you need to: *"I am allowed to pause before I sprint."*

CLOSING ARGUMENT

Urgency will never fire itself. There will always be someone who wants it now, who labels everything time-sensitive, who rewards you for burning yourself down in the name of being "on it." You don't have to live that way.

You can:
• let some emails wait,
• let some "emergencies" age overnight,
• let some smoke clear before you declare a fire.

You can trade being the fastest responder for being the calmest presence in the room. That's the lawyer people actually trust. The tyranny of urgency doesn't end when your inbox calms down. It ends the moment you decide that not everything gets to own your heartbeat. And from that moment on, urgency becomes what it was always meant to be: an occasional mode, not your permanent address.

COURT ORDERS

1. The Urgency Audit (Daily, One Week)
For seven days, track:

- What felt urgent.
- Whether immediate response actually changed the result.
- What you sacrificed to answer fast: *sleep, focus, presence with your people.*

By the end of the week, you'll start recognizing the repeat offenders:

- certain senders
- certain phrases
- certain stories you tell yourself when your phone lights up.

That's not data to shame you.
It's data to free you.

2. The 2x2 Grid
Draw a simple grid:

Top row: Urgent / Not Urgent
Side column: Important / Not Important

Now take an honest look at your week and map your tasks. Then deliberately shift more time into:

Important but *NOT* urgent.

That's where strategy happens, deep work lives, your career-*and sanity*-actually grow. No partner, client, or judge will ever protect that box for you. You are the only one who can.

EXHIBIT SEVENTEEN

The Weight of Comparison

> *Comparison is the thief of joy.*
>
> —Theodore Roosevelt
>
> *Never billed an hour in his life, but still knew what he was talking about.

BACKGROUND

We were three rounds into a law school alumni happy hour when the scoreboard in my head lit up. I hadn't seen these people in a decade. By the time the fries hit the table, I'd tallied who made partner, who went in-house, who argued at the Illinois Supreme Court, who pivoted into a startup, and who looked like they hadn't slept since the bar exam. No one said we were competing. But the air had that tight shimmer of quiet math.

Every "How are things going?" arrived with the unspoken translation: *Are you winning?* I could hear myself answering with facts that sounded fine on paper and somehow felt insufficient leaving my mouth.

That's the gravity of comparison, take what you've built, however meaningful, and make it feel small next to someone else's scaffolding. If control is the illusion and perfection is the prison, comparison is the parasite. Lawyers live on a constant scoreboard, who:

- *made partner first?*
- *has the corner office?*
- *has the bigger book?*

- *has the shinier LinkedIn post?*
- *has the client roster with names that impress people who don't even know what those companies do?*

We measure ourselves not by our own progress, but by everyone else's highlight reel, then wonder why the climb feels so heavy. It's not the hill. It's the weight you added to your pack when you decided their summit was your benchmark.

The parasite is subtle. It doesn't shout; it whispers. You open LinkedIn "just to check what's new" and suddenly you're litigating your life against a stranger's milestone.

You hear a classmate argued en banc and your win from last week feels like a scrimmage. A peer's "thrilled to share" post about joining a board turns your steady leadership into a participation trophy in your own mind. None of the facts changed. Only the frame did.

That's how parasites work: they steal nutrition from whatever you've fed yourself and leave you hungry. The silent competition has its rituals.

"Coffee to catch up?" becomes a deposition where both parties only ask questions they already know the answers to.

"How's the team?" means "How big is your headcount?" "How's work-life balance?" means "How many hours are you billing?" "Any fun travel?" means "Can you afford it?"

No one is trying to be cruel. Most of us are trying to locate ourselves in a profession that rarely tells the truth about enough. But the subtext piles up until even good news tastes like ash because it isn't as good as someone else's.

It's worse because law bakes comparison into the crust. Rankings. Chambers. Super Lawyers. Vault. League tables for deals, for cases, for matters no civilian has ever heard of.

We build bios like box scores and wrap our worth in bullet points. Clients ask about track records. Firms elevate on metrics. The incentives aren't imaginary. But living by them alone turns your life into an exhibit list curated for a jury that never convenes.

Here's the part we miss while refreshing the feed: their facts aren't your facts. Their case isn't your case. Comparison is like citing opposing counsel's brief as your own authority. At best it's persuasive, and often not even that. You don't know the exhibits that didn't make their post: what it cost, what broke, what was quietly traded away to get the corner office or the headline. You're comparing your record, with all its sealed filings, to the public version of theirs. That's not argument. That's aspiration dressed up as evidence.

I wish I could say I'm immune now. I still catch the itch. A peer lands a glossy media hit and I feel a flicker of "behind." Someone younger steps into a role I had to bull my way toward and a petty voice mutters about timelines. Then I remember the train ride home after that happy hour: how I felt smaller than I am because I was running numbers on a game I don't even want to play. I don't want their life. I want mine, lived on purpose, not narrated by a chorus of imagined judges.

What loosens the parasite's grip isn't pretending you don't care. It's caring about the right record. What's really in your case file? The people who trust you with hard work because you tell them the truth. The kid who still checks the stands for your eyes. The colleague who breathes easier when you walk into the room. The mornings you chose presence over performance. The boundaries you honored. The craft you kept clean when shortcuts were cheap. None of that will trend. All of it counts.

When I look back at that reunion now, what I remember most isn't who "won." It's the moment the conversation slipped into real life: someone admitted a rough year, someone else talked about a parent's decline, someone spoke about the challenges of being a first-time parent, another about leaving practice because being a whole person mattered more than another notch. For a second, the parasite lost reception. No metrics. No trophies. Just people, complicated and honest. I left lighter, not because I'd climbed the imaginary ladder, but because I'd climbed down from it.

There's a cleaner way to keep score, if you insist on a score at all: Am I becoming someone I respect? Is my work aligned with what I say matters? Do the people who know me best feel more seen or more managed? Did I trade my presence for optics today, or the other way around? Those questions don't fit neatly in a bio. They do fit in a life.

Comparison will always knock. Let it. You don't have to invite it in and build it a guest room. You can note the pang, bless the other person's path without making it your precedent, and return to your own facts.

Progress measured against your former self isn't as flashy as a metrics dashboard, but it's honest. And unlike the highlight reel, it's yours.

DISCOVERY REQUEST

Whose success have you been treating as evidence against your own, and what would happen if you withdrew that case?

- *Make it concrete.*
- *Name the person.*
- *Name the circumstance.*

Then picture yourself striking that exhibit from the record—no drama, no argument, just a quiet administrative action:

"This no longer applies."

Sometimes the cleanest relief isn't winning the comparison. It's dismissing it.

OBJECTIONS

Objection No. 1
"But comparison motivates me."

Sustained—with limits. Yes, seeing others succeed can light a fire. But if the fire keeps burning your house down, it's not motivation, it's arson. Comparison sharpens when used sparingly. Used constantly, it erodes your internal compass until you're performing your life instead of living it.

Objection No. 2
"But if I don't compare, how do I know I'm doing well?"

Overruled. Benchmarks matter. But they are reference points, not identity documents. You don't need someone else's win to validate your worth.

You need alignment:
Does my life feel like mine?
Does my progress match my values?
That's not comparison. That's clarity.

RULING & RELIEF REQUESTED

Ruling

Comparison is dismissed for lack of standing. It has no jurisdiction over the truth of your life, your values, or your trajectory.

Motion for Immediate Relief

Tonight, open your Daily Docket for Peace. List three ordinary moments from today that made your life unmistakably yours. No milestones. No trophies. Just the stuff that actually keeps you standing.

SETTLEMENT TERMS

- Other people's lives are persuasive authority, not binding precedent.
- Comparison alters the record and distorts the evidence.
- Joy becomes admissible the moment you stop trying to outrun someone else's metrics.
- The only score that matters: Am I becoming someone I respect?

CLOSING ARGUMENT

Comparison is a weight disguised as motivation. It bends your posture, narrows your vision, and convinces you you're losing a race you never agreed to run. Your life isn't a scoreboard. It isn't a verdict. It isn't a competition. It's a story, your story, and the only meaningful judgment is this:

Do I like the life I'm actually living?
If the answer is even a quiet, imperfect yes, you're already ahead where it matters.

COURT ORDERS

1. Social Media Cross-Examination
Find a post that stings. Then interrogate it:

What facts are missing?
What's the spin?
What doesn't this person show?
Why am I assuming their headline tells the whole story?

Nine times out of ten, the gloss melts. You're comparing your raw footage to their curated reel.

2. Limit Scorekeeping to Your Own Growth
Any time you catch yourself tallying someone else's stats, pause and *ask*:

"Is this my game to score?"
If not, drop it. Your life isn't played on their field.

3. Add to Your Peace Contract
Write it somewhere visible:

"My life is not in competition."

This clause is binding.
No amendments permitted.

EXHIBIT EIGHTEEN

The Illusion of Balance

> *Balance is not better time management, but better boundary management. Balance means making choices and enjoying those choices.*
>
> —Betsy Jacobson
>
> *probably never tried to bill 2,000 hours a year.

BACKGROUND

I tried to buy balance with tickets. Three straight weeks of late-night prep for trial: the kind of run where you live on energy drinks and anxiety-induced adrenaline. Closing arguments wrapped, I grabbed seats to a Marvel arena show for my son and me as a make-good. Dad time, loud and shiny. I told myself this was the counterweight.

During the first act, I kept refreshing my phone for updates: pre-trial motion watch, client texts, partner pings. When I finally looked up, my son was looking at me, face lit by the screen I was supposed to be ignoring. Balance didn't save me. Presence would have.

Ask any lawyer how they're doing, and you'll hear some variation of: *I'm just trying to find balance.* Balance between work and home. Between ambition and sanity. Between the part of you that loves the chase and the part that wants to throw your phone in Lake Michigan. But here's the truth: balance is mostly a myth.

We picture it like an elegant set of scales: billables on one side, family dinners on the other. Perfectly level, a still life you can maintain with the right planner and a few hacks. Real life laughs at that. The scales are rigged. Cases explode. Kids get sick. Judges set hearings on birthdays. Clients escalate because they're scared and call it urgency. Partners forward you the six most stressful words in the profession, "Can you take a quick look?" at 10:58 p.m.

There's no steady equilibrium. There's shifting weight and constant recalibration, a seesaw in the wind.

Balance sells because it promises a permanent solution to a moving problem. It suggests you can engineer a life where nothing spills. So, we try to spreadsheet our way there. We carve the week into neat blocks and then watch Tuesday detonate by 9:40 a.m. We promise a "light Friday" and spend it rescheduling Monday. We plan a clean vacation and spend the first three days detoxing from phantom pings.

The more we chase balance as a fixed state, the more we feel like failures for living in gravity.

What we have isn't balance; it's a portfolio. Some days, you prioritize work because the moment calls for it. Some days, you prioritize home because the moment matters more. Some seasons are heavy by design (trial, closing, crisis), and the only honest move is to acknowledge the heaviness and plan your recovery like you plan your filings.

Other seasons invite breath, and if you don't take it, the calendar will happily rent your capacity to the next "urgent" thing. Balance as an aesthetic is brittle. Allocation as a practice bends and survives.

The trap inside "finding balance" is how it slides into performance. You start staging proof: a selfie from the field trip you barely attended, a Saturday at the park haunted by a to-do list, a family night out that you narrate like an exhibit for a judge who never arrives. You end up everywhere and nowhere, present enough to be counted, absent enough to be missed.

That Marvel night was exactly that. I showed up physically and vanished mentally. I thought I was buying back what the trial had taken. I paid for seats and brought a ghost.

Perfection makes balance worse. If your standard is to look good at work and look good at life all the time, you'll spend both pretending. You'll nod through bedtime while drafting tomorrow's answers in your head. You'll smile at dinner while rehearsing the partner's critique.

You'll live in the mental control tower, forever managing optics. The people around you won't get you; they'll get your performance. And performance, even loving performance, runs out of oxygen.

The antidote isn't to swing hard the other way and pretend work doesn't matter. It does. Clients deserve seriousness. Teams need leaders who show up. Courts run on attendance. The shift is subtler: from balancing to choosing. Choosing what carries weight today. Choosing what gets a no without apology. Choosing presence over optics in whatever you've chosen. It's less impressive on paper. It's far more alive in practice.

What does that look like when it's not social media? It looks like telling a client, "We'll turn this by tomorrow, tonight I'm offline," and letting the sentence stand without a paragraph of justification. It looks like leaving on time on a Wednesday with nothing "special" as cover. It looks like taking the heavy season seriously and then, when it ends, truly ending it, no victory lap in your inbox to prove how committed you are. It looks like saying yes to a kid's slow story and no to a meeting that only exists because someone is anxious and needs a place to put it. It looks like drawing a small circle around one hour and guarding it like a hearing. It looks like admitting when the scales have tipped for too long and rebalancing with action, not slogans.

There's a legal metaphor I trust here more than the polished scale: proportionality. We use it to decide what discovery is appropriate given the stakes, the resources, the issues. The point isn't to make both sides equal; it's to make the effort fit the matter. Apply that to a life. Some days merit a sprint; others merit a walk. Some fights deserve everything you've got; others deserve to die quietly in draft. Trying to make all of it equal will break you. Right-sizing it might save you.

I think about my son in that seat looking at me as if to ask, "You're checking your email again?" more than I think about the trial we'd just finished. Not because it was a morality tale, but because it made the math undeniable.

The thing I was protecting (reputation, responsiveness, the illusion that I'm always "on it") wasn't as valuable as the exact minute I traded away. There was no audience to applaud the refresh button; there was a kid who wanted a witness. Balance would have been a picture. Presence was the point.

So, no: I'm not "finding balance." I'm practicing allocation and fidelity. Allocation: giving the right thing the right weight for the season I'm in. Fidelity: being true to whatever I chose. If it's the brief, write it; if it's the game, watch it. Some weeks I'll tip one way on purpose. Some weeks I'll tip the other. The myth says a good lawyer keeps it all level. The truth is a decent human learns to adjust without turning the people they love into counterweights.

The scales are rigged. The calendar is rude. The profession will rarely help you. But you get a vote in how you spend the minutes inside the mess. Balance is a marketing word. Presence is a practice. And the only proof that practice needs is a life that feels less like a performance and more like a room you can finally stand in.

DISCOVERY REQUEST

Where are you chasing balance, when what you really need is permission to lean? Name the area (work, parenting, partnership, health, rest, ambition) and be blunt:

Are you aiming for symmetry?
Or are you asking for permission to stop feeling guilty?

Balance is the spreadsheet fantasy. Leaning is the human reality.

OBJECTIONS

Objection No 1:
"But without balance, I'll burn out."

Sustained—with clarification. Burnout is real. But balance isn't the antidote, boundaries are.

You don't need a perfectly level life. You need a life where you can say:

"This matters now. That can wait."

Balance demands performance. Boundaries make room for humanity.

Objection No. 2
"If I stop aiming for balance, won't everything fall apart?"

Overruled. Things fall apart sometimes, whether you chase balance or not. The trick isn't to keep everything level. It's to release the illusion that you can. Balance tries to hold the world still. Presence lets you live in the world that exists.

RULING & RELIEF REQUESTED

Ruling

The illusion of balance is struck from the record as an unworkable theory. Life is not a scale; it's a moving docket. A good lawyer recalibrates. A whole human does too.

Motion for Immediate Relief

Draft your Boundary Brief tonight.
One line. One boundary. Enforceable.

Examples:
"I don't check email after 8 p.m."
"If I'm at the game, I'm at the game."
"No meetings during lunch unless someone's bleeding or fired."

Small. Clear. Human.

SETTLEMENT TERMS

- Balance is an illusion of symmetry in a world built on motion.
- Boundaries protect what balance only pretends to manage.
- Presence—not perfection—is the real equilibrium.
- You are allowed to tilt.
- You are allowed to tilt back.

CLOSING ARGUMENT

Balance is not the prize. Presence is. Boundaries are. Flow is. You don't need to live like a scale, forever measuring, adjusting, performing. You need to live like a story: sometimes weighted, sometimes messy, always yours.

Let go of balance. Tilt toward what matters. And trust yourself to tilt back when the season shifts.

COURT ORDERS

1. The Tilt Test (Weekly)
Each Sunday night, *ask*:

Where do I need to tilt this week?
Work?
Family?
Rest?
Recovery?
Creativity?

Declare the tilt. Then lean, with intention, not apology. You can't stay upright all the time. You can stay honest.

2. Replace "Balance" With "Presence"
Your new vocabulary:

"I'm setting boundaries."
"I'm choosing presence."
"I'm allocating my energy."

Language is precedent. Use better law.

3. Add to Your Peace Contract
Write it where you'll see it:

"I will not measure my life in hours but in moments fully lived."

This clause is permanent. No amendments allowed.

EXHIBIT NINETEEN

The Addiction to Achievement

> *It is amazing what you can accomplish if you do not care who gets the credit.*
>
> —Harry S. Truman

BACKGROUND

The first time I argued and won a major motion, the adrenaline hit like a clean shot to the vein. For days I walked taller, chest light, brain humming at a frequency that made food taste better and stairs feel optional. I told myself I'd unlocked the secret to life: win big, feel big. Colleagues nodded a little longer in the hallways. A partner said, "Nice work," in that dry way that counts as a parade in our world. I slept like a champion for two nights, and then the strangest thing happened.

I woke up craving another hearing, another fight, another cliff to leap and land. The high wore off. The hook stayed in.

If balance is an illusion, achievement is the drug that keeps us chasing it anyway. Lawyers are high-functioning addicts. Our substance of choice isn't caffeine or alcohol (though I know many lawyers who enjoy one or both a bit too much). It's achievement.

The hit of closing the deal. The rush of winning the motion. The applause, spoken or silent, when someone calls us indispensable. It feels good. Until it owns you.

You know you're using when the calendar becomes a dispenser. You don't see clients and matters; you see potential doses. That TRO? A quick bump. That summary judgment? A weekend bender. That "great job" in the all-hands? Micro-dose to get through the afternoon. You tell yourself this is ambition, professionalism, devotion to craft. Sometimes it is. Often, it's the simplest transaction in the world: I give you victory; you give me permission to feel like I exist.

Here's the problem with addiction: tolerance builds. The same win that once felt like Everest becomes Tuesday. The same "we couldn't have done this without you" that made your month becomes baseline tone. You recalibrate without noticing. The bar moves higher; the satisfaction window shrinks. I once closed a 1.5 billion dollar transaction. By the next morning, I was already asking, What's next? No celebration, no pause, just the itch. Achievement had stopped being a milestone and become a fix.

It sounds ridiculous from the outside. From the inside, it feels like survival. If productivity is your oxygen and praise your blood sugar, standing still feels like suffocation. That's how you end up refreshing email at your kid's game, manufacturing urgency at 11:47 p.m., volunteering for "just one more" because the cavity behind your ribs won't sit quietly without a new hit.

The work benefits, for a while. Then the edges fray. Judgment gets noisy. Everything becomes a vehicle for validation, and if it won't drive you to the feeling fast enough, you push it until it breaks.

Achievement is slippery because it looks like virtue. Clients love closers. Firms promote winners. Bios are scoreboards by design. If you're not careful, the pursuit that once served your craft starts eating your life and calling it "standards."

You mistake frequency for excellence, volume for mastery, motion for meaning. You start editing other people's work not because it's wrong but because it doesn't deliver the micro-hit of sounding like you. You start saying yes to matters that don't fit because empty space feels dangerous. You construct a day where the only relief available is the next notch.

The withdrawal is quiet and mean. It shows up on the backside of a big result as a feeling that the room has gone gray. People congratulate you and you nod like someone who has already moved apartments in the night. You tell yourself you're hungry, driven, laser-focused.

Maybe. Or maybe you're just unable to metabolize "enough" without a fresh infusion. The body knows the difference. One fuels you; the other keeps you jittering across the surface of your own life.

There's also the collateral damage. Teams learn your appetite and start feeding it: escalations framed as emergencies, easy wins stacked so you can stay "hot," nights and weekends gladly sacrificed because the god of outcome demands smoke. At home, the ledger grows unbalanced.

You become a person who can attend a game without being present, who can schedule a vacation and convert it into a remote office with better views, who can tell a partner, "After this one, I'll slow down," and mean it until the calendar coughs up the next altar.

I don't have a tidy miracle to sell you. What changed for me wasn't a vow to stop caring; it was a recognition that the high was grading my work for me, and it was a terrible grader. It gave A's to anything that produced applause and quietly failed the quiet, durable choices that make you someone worth trusting: telling a client the sober truth when a "win" would be a mirage, letting a junior lawyer own a moment even if it cost me a spotlight, walking away from a term sheet that could close but shouldn't. Those didn't flood the system. They steadied it.

The strangest part of stepping back from the drip is how ordinary the world remains. The cases keep coming. Some you win. Some you don't. People who valued you for the right reasons keep valuing you. People who needed you to be a fireworks display drift toward someone more explosive. The noise lowers. The craft returns. The minutes between hits, once unbearable, start to feel like a place you can live.

I still love achievement. I still chase outcomes. I still feel that jolt when a strategy lands, the CEO agrees, or a negotiation clicks into place. But I try not to confuse the chemical with the meaning. The meaning is the craft, the people, the integrity of the choices made along the way. The meaning is the life that exists on either side of the hearing, the deal, the email, the life that doesn't care how many zeros were in the headline so long as you showed up for dinner with your eyes.

The high promised me freedom and delivered dependency. The work didn't demand that; I did. What I keep learning, on good days, the hard way on others, is that the only win that truly lasts is the one where I don't trade away the rest of my life to feel it. When the rush comes, I let it pass. When the silence follows, I try to stay. Not to prove anything. Just to remember what being unhooked sounds like.

DISCOVERY REQUEST

What would success look like if no one else ever knew about it? Strip out the applause, the optics, the resumé line, the performance review, the "thrilled to announce" post.

- *What remains?*
- *What matters?*
- *What actually feels like success to you*—not to an imaginary audience?

That answer is the first crack in the addiction.

OBJECTIONS

Objection No. 1
"But achievement pays the bills."

Sustained. Yes—achievement keeps the lights on. But obsession isn't the same as ambition. When your identity depends entirely on the next win, you're not earning anymore, you're dosing. You're chasing a feeling, not building a life. Achievement is income. Validation is a habit. Only one of those deserves to run your calendar.

Objection No. 2
"But ambition is what got me here."

Overruled. Ambition built the résumé. Addiction erodes the person reading it. There's a difference between rising and white-knuckling your way through every day because silence feels like failure. You don't need to kill your ambition. You need to stop letting it live in your bloodstream.

RULING & RELIEF REQUESTED

Ruling

Achievement is hereby reclassified as an occasional exhibit, not evidence of worth. Wins are data points, not diagnoses. Milestones, not medicine. Your value is not measured in verdicts, deals, closings, or applause.

Motion for Immediate Relief

Begin your Achievement Fast tomorrow morning. Log your quiet wins, but do not perform them. No humblebrags. No broadcasts. No performative announcements. Just notice your own success without importing an audience.

It will feel itchy. That's withdrawal. That's the point.

SETTLEMENT TERMS

- Achievement is a milestone, not a mood stabilizer.
- Validation is optional, not oxygen.
- Rest isn't negligence; it's recovery.
- You can still pursue excellence without becoming dependent on applause.

CLOSING ARGUMENT

Achievement isn't the enemy. But when it becomes the only way you feel alive, it stops being success and starts being a cage. You don't need another deal, another verdict, another attaboy to justify your existence. You don't need to sprint from high to high to avoid the quiet in between. You don't need to prove what was already true before you ever won a motion. You were worthy before the victories. You remain worthy after them. Stop living for the next hit. Start living for your actual life.

COURT ORDERS

1. No Achievement Posts for Seven Days
Not even the "quick update" variety. Let your accomplishments live privately, like something sacred. Teach your brain that success doesn't require spectators.

2. One Quiet Win Per Day (Non-Work)
Identify and honor one win each day that has nothing to do with your job:

- *Taking a walk.*
- *Listening to your kid's full story without multitasking.*
- *Cooking a meal.*
- *Going to bed on time.*
- *Saying no without writing a novel of justification.*

Celebrate these small wins like they're verdicts.
This is how you rewire where "enough" comes from.

3. Add to Your Peace Contract
Write it clearly:
"My worth is not contingent on outcomes."

Post it where your eyes land before your ego wakes up.

EXHIBIT TWENTY

Surrender is Not Defeat

> *Give me the grace to accept with serenity the things that cannot be changed, courage to change the things which should be changed, and the wisdom to distinguish the one from the other.*
>
> —The Serenity Prayer
>
> *Recited in courtrooms, kitchens, and recovery meetings alike.

BACKGROUND

I stayed on a case long after the facts had buried us. Let me be clear. You don't get to just drop off a case, but long before the case was over, I knew we were likely done.

You could feel it in the record: cold, uncooperative, immune to charm. I kept writing memos anyway, folding logic into origami, filing motions I knew were dead on arrival, rehearsing arguments that sounded persuasive mostly because I needed them to. I told myself I was being zealous. Really, I was refusing reality because I couldn't stomach the word concede. We lost, of course. The ruling hurt.

But the real defeat wasn't the order; it was the weeks I spent denying what was already true, bleeding time and sleep and judgment because surrender felt like failure. Surrender would have freed me sooner. My fear of it only prolonged the suffering.

Lawyers are allergic to the word surrender. It sounds weak. Passive. Like giving up. We're trained to fight, argue, and appeal until the final breath. The cultural script is simple: push harder, outwork fate, outthink gravity. But here's the paradox we hate to say out loud: the more you fight what can't be changed, the more defeated you feel. The more you practice surrender (not apathy, not laziness, but conscious release), the stronger you become. Surrender isn't waving the white flag. It's putting down the sword that's cutting your own hand.

You can hear the allergy in our language. We rename surrender to make it palatable: "strategic pivot," "resource allocation," "reframing." Anything but let go. Yet, the body knows. You wake up clenched. You narrate the day like a closing argument you must win. You keep a doomed settlement on life support because endings bruise your identity. You work nights to "keep momentum" on a deal whose math only works in a model. You press a witness who breaks worse with every prep. None of that is strength. It's fear in a suit.

Surrender, practiced honestly, clarifies. It draws a jurisdictional line between what belongs to you and what belongs to the world. Judges set schedules you won't move. Markets turn. A client chooses a path you advised against. Someone you love decides to leave. You can spend weeks trying to litigate reality or you can lay down the fantasy that force equals control and reclaim what's still yours: your ethics, your preparation, your tone, your next right move.

I learned the lesson again when I realized I needed to leave my law firm job. It was just two years after I made partner and people thought I was crazy. I fought the truth for months, negotiating with reality like it was a contract: maybe if I do more; maybe if I fix myself; maybe if I just push harder. I stacked fresh goals on a hollow foundation and called it grit. All I did was delay the inevitable.

The day I finally said, it's over, and that's okay, I braced for collapse. Instead, I felt strength. It was like setting down a case file I'd been carrying for miles. Surrender didn't destroy me. It returned the energy I needed for the next chapter, one that redefined my career, my peace, and my definition of success.

What makes surrender feel so dangerous is the story underneath: if I stop pushing, I'm exposed. If I stop managing, I'm ordinary. If I accept this, I'll never win again. The opposite is closer to the truth.

When you stop arguing with the river, you finally have hands free to steer the boat. When you stop spending yourself on impossibilities, you gain capacity for the fights that matter. Teams relax because they're not being conscripted into your denial. Clients trust you more because your advice isn't colored by your ego's need to rescue the day. People at home get a person back instead of a performance.

There's also the practical math. Fighting un-winnable battles consumes premium bandwidth (your best attention, your calm, your creativity) and returns nothing but scorch. Surrender reallocates those resources.

On that buried case, the moment we stopped, we could protect the client's next move, salvage relationships, and write a clean record of why not that preserved credibility in the only court that matters long-term: the court of trust. When I left the firm, the day after the "collapse" looked remarkably like a beginning. The air had oxygen again. My work got straighter. Decisions simplified: less noise, more signal.

We confuse fighting with virtue because law often rewards push. Sometimes it should. There are emergencies that call for teeth and bone. But a life calibrated to permanent combat is a life built on misread jurisdiction. You are not the current. You are the boat. You can steer, trim the sail, and read the water. You do not command the river. Surrender is the moment you stop pretending you do.

If you need a diagnostic, listen for these tells: You keep drafting clever instead of writing true. You present options you don't believe in because conceding would bruise your image. You call persistence what your calendar would call compulsion. You revisit decisions already rendered by reality (by the judge, by the market, by the other person's choice) and spend hours polishing arguments that cannot land. That's not diligence. That's a refusal to accept that endings are part of the job and part of being alive.

What replaces the fight isn't nothing; it's proportion. You still prepare hard where preparation matters. You still argue where arguments can move the needle. You still stay up late when the cause warrants it. You just stop setting yourself on fire to prove you're brave.

You stop equating suffering with integrity. You stop treating every loss as a referendum on your right to belong.

I go back to the moment a partner skimmed my three pages of clever and asked the gentlest, most devastating question in the profession: "What if we stop?" I heard it like a bell. We did. The sky didn't fall. The judge arrived at the same place, only cleaner. The client respected the call. The team slept. And later, when a winnable matter came through the door, we had a full tank.

Surrender won't earn applause in an all-firm email. There's no trophy for "We chose not to grind ourselves to dust for optics." What it gives you is quieter and more durable: time you would have burned trying to bully the inevitable, steadiness in rooms that mistake speed for competence, the ability to lose without losing yourself and to win without mistaking force for skill.

I still feel the flinch when a matter tilts against me. The old reflex reaches for the sword. Most days now, I notice the edge before it finds my hand. I remember the case that needed to die, the job that needed to end, the strength that arrived when I set both down. Surrender isn't defeat. It's consent to reality. It's not quitting the field; it's choosing a winnable one. In a profession crowded with battles that never asked for our heroics, that choice is the rarest kind of power—the kind that leaves you whole enough to keep showing up.

DISCOVERY REQUEST

What would you gain, not lose, if you stopped fighting the un-winnable case? Don't overthink it. Name the case (literal or not). Name the cost. Name the freedom waiting on the other side. This is about honesty, not heroics.

Legal Metaphor Break

Think of surrender as stipulating to uncontested facts. You're not rolling over. You're acknowledging what's already true, so you can focus on what still matters. That's not weakness. That's strategy.

OBJECTIONS

Objection No. 1
"If I surrender, I'll lose credibility."

Overruled. Clarity builds credibility. Integrity builds credibility. Knowing when to stop builds credibility. People don't trust the lawyer who fights every single issue. They trust the one who knows when the record is closed.

Objection No. 2
"Surrender feels like letting people down."

Sustained—with clarification. Yes, someone might be disappointed. But you're not responsible for fueling their fantasy that you can fix the unfixable. You're responsible for staying sane, steady, and whole. Sometimes the kindest move, for them and for you, is saying, *Enough.*

The Real Strength of Surrender:

- It frees you from the illusion of control.
- It redirects energy from denial to presence.
- It creates space where peace can return.

Surrender isn't collapse. It's clarity.

RULING & RELIEF REQUESTED

Ruling
The illusion of control is dismissed with prejudice.

Motion for Immediate Relief
Complete your Surrender List tonight. Mark one ongoing fight "Surrendered."

Ask the only questions that matter:
Am I fighting because this is winnable?
Or because I'm afraid of what it means if I stop?

Then mark it: *Surrendered.* Feel what opens when you stop pretending you can brute-force fate.

SETTLEMENT TERMS

- Surrender is not weakness-it's wisdom.
- You cannot out-argue reality.
- Peace requires dropping cases you can't win.

CLOSING ARGUMENT

Surrender is not defeat. Defeat is clinging to battles long after the judgment has entered. Surrender is clarity. It's the honest jurisdictional line between what belongs to you and what never did. You don't lose by letting go. You win something far rarer in this profession: a life not lived in perpetual combat. Strength isn't in the next swing of the sword. It's in the open hand.

COURT ORDERS

1. The Hand Drop Exercise
Each day:

Pick up a pen, stress ball, anything small.
Grip it tight. Notice the strain. Then open your hand. Let it fall. That's surrender. Not a speech. Not a ceremony. Just release.

2. Stipulate to Uncontested Facts
Once a day, in work or life, *say*:
"This part is already true."

No argument. No resistance. No appeal. It trains the muscle you've been avoiding.

3. Add to Your Peace Contract
Write it clearly:
"I will stop appealing verdicts that life has already rendered."

This is your new rule of life. Treat it as binding.

PART V

Closing Argument & Letter from The Author

CLOSING ARGUMENT

Members of the Jury.

Picture the courtroom of your own life. You're at the counsel table with files stacked, exhibits scattered, a jury of your peers watching. But this isn't a trial about your client. It is about you.

You've acted as though you are the entire system: judge, jury, clerk, bailiff, opposing counsel, and client. You've convinced yourself the courthouse would crumble if you let go for even a moment.

You've been preparing, presenting, objecting, and sentencing all at once, and it has exhausted you.This book has been our trial.

Together, we've presented evidence, raised objections, and examined witnesses: your memories, my stories, our shared habits. And now, at closing, it's time to summarize the case.

EXHIBIT ONE: *The Cult of Control.*

We learned that lawyers are trained to grip everything: to anticipate disaster, script every outcome, and mistake control for safety. The evidence showed otherwise: control is a mirage. Worry doesn't prevent disaster. It only erases presence.

EXHIBIT TWO: *Perfection Is a Prison.*

We saw how the chase for flawless work steals hours, strains relationships, and still never satisfies. Perfection isn't excellence; it's self-erasure.

EXHIBIT THREE: *The Counsel or Trap.*

We carry "counsel" into every room, advising when we should listen, fixing when we should feel. The result? Intimacy dies on the stand.

EXHIBIT FOUR: *Over-Responsibility Is Ego.*

What masquerades as generosity is often pride: the belief that only we can hold it all together.

EXHIBIT FIVE: *Your Brain on Law.*

The neurological evidence was clear: law rewires the mind. Hyper-vigilance, rumination, adversarial thinking: tools that serve the client, but sabotage peace if left unchecked.

By Exhibits Six through Ten, the record expanded. We introduced the pause: the breath between stimulus and response. We accepted the uncontrollable. We learned that losing doesn't make us losers. We remembered that not every email deserves a reply.

In Exhibits Eleven through Fourteen, the testimony turned toward sufficiency. Enough is not laziness. Enough is sanity. Enough is choosing presence over polish, humanity over performance.

And in Exhibits Fifteen through Twenty, we dismantled illusions. Someday is a myth. Urgency is theater. Comparison is irrelevant evidence. Balance is impossible. Achievement is an addiction. And surrender, far from weakness, is freedom. Together, these exhibits tell one story: carrying everything doesn't make us excellent. It makes us brittle.

Throughout, I've placed myself on the stand. I told you about missing my daughter's shot for an email no one read. About the collapse in my car after a sixteen-hour day. About the family who needed a father, not a lawyer. But I also told you about the quieter wins. The silence that saved a negotiation. The Friday I left at six. The pizza nights. The laughter. The moments when joy became admissible again. That is my testimony. But this case isn't about me. It's about you.

We've heard the usual objections:

"But this is what makes me good."
Sustained—in part.

Good lawyering requires vigilance at
work, not omnipotence everywhere.

"But letting go lowers the bar."
Overruled.

Letting go isn't apathy; it is discernment.
It's refusing to waste energy on what
was never your responsibility.

"But my clients expect perfection."
Overruled.

Clients expect competence, clarity, and care.
Not your life as collateral.

"If I don't carry it all, everything collapses."
Overruled.

The system never depended on you being the whole thing. That belief is ego disguised as duty.

The objections have been heard. They are overruled. When I look back, I can cross-examine my own record.

Why did you equate exhaustion with excellence? Because I thought collapse was the price of success.

Why did you choose perfection over presence? Because I feared judgment more than absence.

Why did you treat joy as irrelevant? Because I believed seriousness was the only admissible evidence. The answers are damning, but clarifying. The cross-examination makes the truth plain: I wasn't serving my clients better by destroying myself. I was serving my fear. The case is simple. Control is a mirage. Perfection is a prison. Over-responsibility is arrogance. Comparison is inadmissible. Exhaustion is not excellence.

Balance is a myth. Surrender is freedom.

The evidence is overwhelming. The verdict is clear. Members of the jury, the record is complete. The case is closed. The verdict is peace. You are not the whole system. You never were. You never will be. But trials end. Life doesn't. After the verdict comes the living. Two things worth a second look on your end:

"Exhibit Three: *The Counsel or Trap*" reads oddly, possibly meant to be "The Counsel Trap"? And "Members of the Jury" opens capitalized but later drops to "the jury," so worth picking one and applying it consistently throughout.

PART V

Letter from the Author

Dear Reader,

If you've made it this far, you've sat through the entire trial. You've heard the case against carrying everything. You've reviewed the exhibits, listened to the objections, and watched them overruled. The verdict has been read: you are not the whole system.

But as every lawyer knows, the gavel doesn't end the work. After closing arguments, once the jury leaves the box, the real labor begins. Orders must be enforced. Agreements must be lived. Judgments must be carried out—day by day. That is where you stand now.

The Closing Argument was my summation; the gathering of evidence, stories, and metaphors that reveal the cost of trying to be everything at once. This letter is something different. It's not argument or evidence.

It's me stepping down from counsel's table to speak plainly, as one lawyer to another. It's an invitation to move beyond understanding and into practice.

This book does not end with a verdict because understanding isn't enough. If we stopped at the Closing Argument, you'd nod, underline a few lines, maybe promise to remember one or two. Then Monday would come. The inbox would ping. The calendar would crowd. And the old habits would resume their cross-examination.

That's why the Notes on the Practice follow. Think of them as your enforcement section—the part of the judgment that tells you not just what the law is, but how it applies. They're not theories. They're applications.

- **The Mantras** interrupt the critic in your head that insists your worth is still on trial.
- **The Micro-Practices** interrupt the reflex that drives you to exhaustion before you notice you're tired.
- **The Journaling Prompts** drag invisible scripts into daylight so you can cross-examine them and write new ones.
- **The Daily Docket for Peace** gives your peace the same structure you already give your cases, so chaos can stop living in your head.
- **The Emergency Toolkit** steadies you when your chest tightens and your breath shortens.
- **Consent Decree: The 30-Day Plan** trains your brain like you once trained your craft: with small, deliberate, daily repetitions.
- **The Peace Clause** is your binding contract with yourself—a clause that finally protects your humanity.

These notes are where the verdict becomes a binding precedent in your own life.

My Invitation to You

Don't just read the Notes. Use them. Scribble in the margins. Whisper the mantras in courthouse hallways. Run the micro-practices between calls. Write your Surrender List on a Post-it and tear it up. Treat the Daily Docket for Peace like your sanity's case file.

You don't need to do them all. Some will feel natural. Others will feel awkward. That's fine. This isn't about performing new habits perfectly. It's about practicing presence, and remembering you can unclench, even for a moment, and then try again tomorrow.

If you try—even in fragments—you'll start to feel lighter. You'll notice that not every email is an emergency. That rest is strategy. That joy is admissible. That peace is not irrelevant evidence—it belongs in the record.

My Hope

I hope this book gave you language for what you've been feeling. I hope it named the exhaustion you've carried in silence. I hope it reminded you that you are not alone. But more than anything, I hope you practice. Because peace is not handed down like a judgment. It is built, enforced, and renewed daily. The Notes on the Practice that follow aren't an appendix. They're the heart of the book. They're the tools I still use. They're the drills I return to when I forget. They're how you make the ruling of this book binding in your own life.

A Final Word

I don't write this letter as someone who has solved it all. I still grip too tightly to somedays. I still confuse urgency with importance. I still feel the pull to prove my worth in rooms that aren't my jury. But now I know this: I can begin again.

And so can you. The trial is over. The case is closed. The verdict is peace. The work now is yours.

The Notes on the Practice that follow are your tools. Use them. Test them. Live them. Draft your Peace Clause and sign it with the same seriousness you bring to every contract you've ever negotiated. Because the ruling of this book is not abstract. It's your life.

With gratitude,
Matthew Campobasso

PART VI

Notes on The Practice

The Lawyer's Toolkit for Letting Go

PART VI

Notes on The Practice
The Lawyer's Toolkit for Letting Go

Members of the Jury, picture the courtroom of your own life. You're at the counsel table with files stacked, exhibits scattered, a jury of your peers watching. But this isn't a trial about your client. It is about you. You've acted as though you are the entire system: judge, jury, clerk, bailiff, opposing counsel, and client. You've convinced yourself the courthouse would crumble if you let go for even a moment. You've been preparing, presenting, objecting, and sentencing all at once, and it has exhausted you.

This book has been our trial. Together, we've presented evidence, raised objections, and examined witnesses—your memories, my stories, our shared habits. And now, at closing, it's time to summarize the case.

My Testimony

Throughout, I've placed myself on the stand. I told you about missing my daughter's shot for an email no one read. About the collapse in my car after a sixteen-hour day. About the family who needed a father, not a lawyer. But I also told you about the quieter wins.

The silence that saved a negotiation. The Friday I left at six. The pizza nights. The laughter. The moments when joy became admissible again. That is my testimony. But this case isn't about me. It's about you. But trials end. Life doesn't. After the verdict comes the living. After the gavel falls comes the work of applying the ruling. That's where we turn next.

After the Verdict: *Notes on the Practice*

What follows isn't more argument. There's no more evidence to enter. This is the sentencing. It is not punitive, it's restorative. The Notes on the Practice are your field manual. Your post-trial memorandum. Your roadmap for living the verdict.

Inside, you'll find:

25 Mantras: Rulings for Daily Sanity
"My worth isn't on trial today." "Rest is strategy."

10 Micro-Practices: Drills to Retrain Your Lawyer Brain.
The Inbox Audit, the Silent Pause, the Surrender List

7 Journaling Prompts: Questions that Surface the Unseen Scripts.

Daily Docket for Peace: A Morning and Evening Routine that structures peace the way law structures order.

Emergency Toolkit: Practical Resets.
the Five-Breath Reset, the Walkout, the Gratitude Docket.

Consent Decree: A 30-Day Letting Go Plan.
One small practice a day for a month, bootcamp for your peace of mind.

Peace Clause: Your Binding Contract with Yourself, declaring that you will no longer practice malpractice against your own life.

The Notes that follow are not philosophy. They are practice. Use them as tools, not ornaments. The mantras, micro-practices, journaling prompts, daily docket, emergency toolkit, 30-day plan, and peace clause are the enforcement section of this book, the part that turns understanding into change.

25 MANTRAS

for Lawyers Who Forget

Words shape worlds. In the courtroom, they sway juries. In contracts, they define obligations. In our private lives, they become the silent scripts we follow without question. Mantras are the counter-scripts. They're quick objections to the lies we tell ourselves. They interrupt the spiral. They remind us that peace is not a theory, it's a ruling you can issue anytime.

Here are twenty-five rulings for when you forget who you are outside the law.

1. *My worth isn't on trial today*
2. *Not every email is an emergency*
3. *Excellence, not perfection*
4. *This is outside my jurisdiction*
5. *I can be excellent without being exhausted*
6. *Pause, then proceed*
7. *Not my circus, not my closing argument*
8. *Enough is enough*
9. *Rest is strategy*
10. *I release the outcome, I honor the effort*
11. *My presence matters more than my polish*
12. *Urgency is not importance*
13. *Comparison is irrelevant evidence*
14. *Letting go is leadership*
15. *Surrender is not defeat*
16. *The case is closed*
17. *I am not the whole system*
18. *Joy is admissible*
19. *I don't need to be right to be real*
20. *Peace over performance*
21. *Progress, not precedent*
22. *I am allowed to be human*
23. *This brief can rest*
24. *One breath, one choice*
25. *Enough already*

Ruling No. 1: My worth isn't on trial today.

Lawyers live like the jury is always deliberating. Every meeting, every silence, every raised eyebrow feels like evidence in *Me v. Everyone Else.* It's exhausting-because you're not just doing the work; you're defending your right to belong. I once stumbled mid-presentation in a board meeting early in my in-house career.

For an hour afterward, I replayed it in my head, certain I'd been silently disbarred from credibility. The truth? No one cared. The jury was entirely in my head.

Finding of Fact:

Your worth is not a verdict. It's a constant.

Objection:

"But feedback is about my worth, isn't it?"

Ruling:

Overruled. Feedback measures performance, not humanity. Work can be critiqued. Worth is untouchable.

Practice:

Before a high-stakes meeting, whisper it: *"My worth isn't on trial today."* Write it atop your notes. Afterward, record one non-work thing that proves your worth-like making your child laugh or showing up for a friend.

Verdict:

The case is closed.

Ruling No. 2: Not every email is an emergency.
The inbox is a slot machine of panic. Every ping feels like sirens. Every "urgent" subject line, a subpoena for your soul. But most emails are noise-sound and fury, signifying nothing.

I once missed half my daughter's basketball game answering a "critical" message. I crafted the perfect four-paragraph reply.
The next morning, the sender responded: *"Thanks, noted."* The fire I thought I was extinguishing? Smoke.

Finding of Fact:
The inbox is not the jury. Stop treating it like one.

***Objection*:**
"If I don't respond immediately, I'll look unprofessional."

***Ruling*:**
Overruled. No one remembers the midnight response. They remember consistent reliability.

***Practice*:**
Before you open your inbox, whisper: *"Not every email is an emergency."* Pick three messages today to delay 24 hours. Notice how little collapses.

***Verdict*:**
Your email speed is not your value.

Ruling No. 3: Excellence, not perfection.
Excellence serves clients. Perfection serves the ego.
Excellence asks, *"Is this strong enough to stand?"*
Perfection demands, *"Does this erase every trace of humanity?"*

I once spent six hours fixing formatting in a brief. Fonts, margins, numbering-all pristine. The judge didn't notice. My kids noticed I wasn't at dinner. That was perfection's tax.

Finding of Fact:
Perfection is an aesthetic. Excellence is a standard. They are not the same statute.

Objection:
"But my reputation depends on precision."

Ruling:
Sustained in part. Excellence requires detail. Perfection requires obsession. Know the difference.

Practice:
Before sending, ask: *"Is this excellent, or am I polishing for polish's sake?"* If excellent, stop. Send. Go home.

Verdict:
Excellence is sustainable. Perfection is a prison.

Ruling No. 4: This is outside my jurisdiction.
Lawyers love jurisdiction-it defines authority. Yet outside work, we act like we hold universal jurisdiction over everyone's moods, outcomes, and the economy. I once lost sleep over a stock market drop, as if my mental litigation could reverse it. I mistook obsession for influence.

Finding of Fact:
Not every motion in life requires your signature.

***Objection*:**
"But caring means I should control it."

***Ruling*:**
Overruled. Caring is human. Control is a delusion.

***Practice*:**
List three things stressing you today. Mark which are outside your jurisdiction. Say aloud: *"Dismissed with prejudice."*

***Verdict*:**
You are not the court of last resort. Some cases aren't yours to hear.

Ruling No. 5: I can be excellent without being exhausted.
The legal profession worships exhaustion. Billable martyrdom. Skipped meals as virtue. Burnout as proof of value. But exhaustion isn't evidence of excellence.

It's Exhibit A for imbalance.
I once bragged about an 80-hour week. Colleagues applauded. Inside, I was hollow. My family saw it. My body knew it. That wasn't excellence-it was collapse.

Finding of Fact:
Fatigue is not a credential.

***Objection*:**
"But excellence requires sacrifice."

***Ruling*:**
Sustained-with limits. Sacrifice is sometimes necessary. Self-destruction is not.

***Practice*:**
When tempted to overextend, ask: *"Would I respect this boundary if it belonged to someone else?"* Then honor it.

***Verdict*:**
You don't have to bleed to prove you're good.

Ruling No. 6: Pause, Then Proceed.

Lawyers are rewarded for speed-quick answers, rapid objections, instant analysis. We mistake velocity for intelligence. But speed without pause creates messes that take twice as long to clean up.

I nearly destroyed a client relationship with a midnight email. I felt attacked and drafted a defensive “Reply All.” Something fatigue or grace made me stop. In the morning, I realized it read as insecure, not competent. The pause saved me.

Finding of Fact:

A one-minute pause costs less than a year of damage control.

Objection:

“Clients expect instant responses.”

Ruling:

Overruled. Clients value clarity more than speed. A thoughtful reply tomorrow beats a panicked one tonight.

Practice:

Before answering a triggering email, set a one-minute timer. Breathe until it ends. Most urges expire faster than the timer.

Verdict:

One pause can preserve years of credibility.

Ruling No. 7: Not My Circus, Not My Closing Argument.
We love drama-especially when we can fix it. Every dispute feels like an invitation. But not every circus is yours to enter. I once "mediated" a feud between two associates over credit. I thought I was helping; I became the villain in both stories. I hadn't been hired as counsel, I'd volunteered as collateral damage.

Finding of Fact:
Every conflict is not your case.

***Objection*:**
"If I don't intervene, I'll seem uncaring."

***Ruling*:**
Overruled. Boundaries are not cruelty; they're clarity.

***Practice*:**
When someone drags you into unnecessary conflict, whisper, *"Not my circus, not my closing argument."* Then exit the tent.

***Verdict*:**
You're not obligated to appear in every ring.

Ruling No. 8: Enough Is Enough.

The finish line in law keeps moving. Partner, GC, C-suite-each title promises peace, then raises the bar. You sprint endlessly toward a horizon that never arrives. When I finally reached the executive suite, I expected fulfillment. Instead, I felt emptier. The bar hadn't disappeared, it had relocated higher.

Finding of Fact:

Peace doesn't show up uninvited; it's declared.

***Objection*:**

"But ambition is good."

***Ruling*:**

Sustained-in moderation. Ambition fuels growth. Unchecked, it devours you.

***Practice*:**

Each Sunday, complete this sentence: "... is enough." Then honor it. Example: "*Leaving by six* is enough."

***Verdict*:**

Enough will never find you. You must rule it into existence.

Ruling No. 9: Rest Is Strategy.
Generals and athletes schedule rest; lawyers treat it as negligence. We act like collapse proves commitment. It doesn't. I once went seven years without a real vacation. When I finally unplugged for a week, nothing burned down-except my old belief that rest was weakness.

Finding of Fact:
Rest is not avoidance; it's fuel.

***Objection*:**
"I can't afford to rest."

***Ruling*:**
Overruled. Burnout costs more than any break ever will.

***Practice*:**
Schedule rest like a deposition. Protect it with the same ferocity. When guilt appears, remind yourself: *"Rest is strategy."*

***Verdict*:**
You don't lose ground by resting, you regain jurisdiction over your life.

Ruling No. 10: I Release the Outcome, I Honor the Effort.
Law trains us to worship results: win the case, close the deal, secure the client. But outcomes are rarely ours to control. Effort is. I once lost the hardest case I'd ever worked. I equated loss with failure until I realized the facts-not my worth-decided the verdict.

Finding of Fact:
Outcomes are public record. Effort is personal integrity.

***Objection*:**
"Clients only care about results."

***Ruling*:**
Sustained-but irrelevant. They get one case. You get a career.

***Practice*:**
Before a major meeting, say, *"I honor the effort."* Afterward, write what you gave, not just what you gained.

***Verdict*:**
Peace lives where effort ends and outcomes are released.

Ruling No. 11: My Presence Matters More Than My Polish.
We polish everything-briefs, résumés, small talk. But polish doesn't connect people; presence does. At a family dinner after endless late nights, I thought showing up was enough. My son later said, "Dad, you didn't hear anything I said." He was right. I'd been physically present, emotionally remote.

Finding of Fact:
Presence creates connection. Polish creates distance.

***Objection*:**
"Professionalism requires polish."

***Ruling*:**
Sustained-in court only. Everywhere else, humanity wins.

***Practice*:**
Before a conversation, silence your phone. Ask one follow-up that proves you listened.

***Verdict*:**
Connection outlasts presentation.

Ruling No. 12: Urgency Is Not Importance.

Law firms thrive on adrenaline. Every ping feels like a four-alarm fire. We confuse motion with meaning. I once spent two days buried in an "urgent" email chain. The problem resolved itself; the truly important work sat untouched.

Finding of Fact:

Urgency screams; importance whispers.

***Objection*:**

"Urgent work gets me noticed."

***Ruling*:**

Overruled. Urgency gets attention; importance earns respect.

***Practice*:**

Before starting a task, ask, *"Urgent or important?"* Choose accordingly.

***Verdict*:**

The loudest issue is rarely the most meaningful.

Ruling No. 13: Comparison Is Irrelevant Evidence.
We're trained to analyze precedent-and then we apply it to our lives. We compare salaries, promotions, and résumés as though other people's facts bind our own case. At a law-school reunion, I quietly ranked classmates by success. Later, one of the "top" lawyers admitted he envied my peace. The scoreboard was fiction.

Finding of Fact:
Comparison is persuasive at best, never binding.

***Objection*:**
"Comparison motivates me."

***Ruling*:**
Sustained-in limited scope. Inspiration is useful; envy is toxic.

***Practice*:**
When envy hits, say aloud, *"Irrelevant evidence."* Then list three things you wouldn't trade from your own life.

***Verdict*:**
Comparison is stricken from the record.

Ruling No. 14: Letting Go Is Leadership.
Micromanagement masquerades as strength but signals fear. True leadership delegates, trusts, and releases control. I once insisted on drafting every section of a key motion. My associate finally asked for a chance. I let go-reluctantly-and she produced something better than I could. The client praised her. I learned.

Finding of Fact:
Hoarding control limits growth-yours and theirs.

***Objection*:**
"If I let go, I'll look weak."

***Ruling*:**
Overruled. Refusing to trust looks weaker.

***Practice*:**
Delegate one task you'd normally clutch. Repeat: *"Letting go is leadership."* Watch capability rise on both sides.

***Verdict*:**
Release is power. Control is fear in disguise.

Ruling No. 15: Surrender Is Not Defeat.
To lawyers, surrender sounds like failure. But surrender isn't collapse-it's clarity. It's recognizing when the facts no longer support the claim. I once clung to a doomed deal, drafting memos no one would read. When it finally died, the relief was palpable. The defeat wasn't the loss-it was the wasted denial.

Finding of Fact:
Acceptance is efficiency. Resistance is self-inflicted billable pain.

***Objection*:**
"Surrender will disappoint people."

***Ruling*:**
Sustained-in emotion only. Disappointment fades; burnout lingers.

***Practice*:**
Write one thing you're fighting but can't fix. Say aloud: *"Surrender is not defeat."* Then put it down.

***Verdict*:**
Defeat is clinging. Surrender is freedom.

Ruling No. 16: The Case Is Closed.

Lawyers are professionals at re-argument. We cross-examine the past in the shower, during the commute, even brushing our teeth. We keep cases open in our heads long after they've been adjudicated in real life. I once replayed a botched cross for weeks, rewriting every question in my mind. It didn't change the record. It only eroded my peace.

Finding of Fact:

Reflection teaches. Rumination prosecutes.

***Objection*:**

"But replaying helps me learn."

***Ruling*:**

Sustained-in part. Review teaches. Reliving tortures.

***Practice*:**

When you catch yourself rearguing, say aloud, *"The case is closed."* Visualize filing the transcript in a cabinet and shutting the drawer. Write one takeaway if you must, then stop.

***Verdict*:**

Closure isn't denial. It's sanity.

Ruling No. 17: I Am Not the Whole System.
The law trains us to feel indispensable. We start acting like we're judge, jury, clerk, and opposing counsel all at once. We convince ourselves the courthouse collapses if we take a day off. I once micro-managed a deal from every angle: negotiations, drafts, even travel logistics. I didn't run the system; I clogged it.

Finding of Fact:
The world runs smoother when you stop over-managing it.

***Objection*:**
"But if I don't do it, no one will."

***Ruling*:**
Overruled. They will-maybe differently, maybe imperfectly, but the docket moves on.

***Practice*:**
When overwhelmed, whisper: *"I am not the whole system."* Delegate one thing. Delay another. Drop a third.

***Verdict*:**
You're a participant, not the infrastructure.

Ruling No. 18: Joy Is Admissible.

We treat joy like irrelevant evidence-colorful but inadmissible. Yet joy restores capacity and credibility. It reminds you why you entered the profession in the first place. I once left work early for ice cream with my kids. I felt guilty. They felt happy. That's Exhibit A for why joy belongs in the record.

Finding of Fact:

Joy is material to the preservation of life and sanity.

***Objection*:**

"But joy makes me look unserious."

***Ruling*:**

Overruled. Joy humanizes. Humans earn trust.

***Practice*:**

Choose one joyful act today-music in chambers, laughter at lunch, sunlight on your walk. Whisper: *"Joy is admissible."* Enter it into evidence.

***Verdict*:**

Joy isn't proof of weakness. It's proof of life.

Ruling No. 19: I Don't Need to Be Right to Be Real.
Lawyers are addicted to accuracy. We correct dinner conversations, debate opinions at parties, and fact-check bedtime stories. But being right often kills connection. I once corrected my partner mid-story at a family gathering. "That's not exactly how it happened." The table went silent. I'd won the facts and lost the moment.

Finding of Fact:
Connection outweighs correctness outside of court.

***Objection*:**
"But accuracy matters."

***Ruling*:**
Sustained-in the courtroom. Overruled everywhere else.

***Practice*:**
When tempted to correct someone, stop. Let them finish. Choose being real over being right.

***Verdict*:**
Connection > correction.

Ruling No. 20: Peace Over Performance.
Performance gets applause. Peace gets you a life. We chase the applause and then wonder why we still feel empty. I once gave a flawless board presentation. Everyone clapped. That same week, I sat quietly on the porch with my kids. No applause-just peace. Guess which one I think of with greater affection?

Finding of Fact:
Peace leaves a longer record than praise.

Objection:
"Performance keeps me employed."

Ruling:
Sustained-but incomplete. Peace keeps you human enough to stay employable.

Practice:
When torn between impressing and resting, whisper: *"Peace over performance."* Take the option that restores calm.

***Verdict*:**
Peace sustains longer than applause ever will.

Ruling No. 21: Progress, Not Precedent.
Law lives by precedent. Life shouldn't. We let old mistakes become binding law, even when the facts have changed. I carried shame from botching an early criminal trial for years. Every future case felt like an appeal of that one mistake. It wasn't precedent-it was bad law I hadn't vacated.

Finding of Fact:
The past is persuasive authority, not binding.

Objection:
"But past errors predict future ones."

Ruling:
Overruled. Only if you treat them as final judgments.

Practice:
When haunted by the past, whisper: *"Progress, not precedent."* Take one small action that proves growth.

Verdict:
You can overrule yourself. The court allows it.

Ruling No. 22: I Am Allowed to Be Human.

Law prizes precision and endurance. But you're not a robot-you're a person wearing a suit. After a brutal trial, I sat in my car and cried. I was embarrassed until I realized: my client wept too, openly. If humanity was allowed for them, it's allowed for me.

Finding of Fact:

Humanity is admissible evidence.

Objection:

"Vulnerability weakens respect."

Ruling:

Overruled. Authenticity strengthens trust.

Practice:

When you err or unravel, whisper: *"I am allowed to be human."* Let the verdict stand.

Verdict:

Humanity isn't misconduct. It's proof of heart.

Ruling No. 23: This Brief Can Rest.
We treat drafts like newborns-fussing, adjusting, never satisfied. But over editing kills clarity and sleep. I once stayed up until 3 a.m. perfecting a “final” draft.

The next morning, I reversed half my edits. The work hadn’t improved; my fatigue had worsened it.

Finding of Fact:
At a certain hour, revision becomes regression.

Objection:
“But one more edit might help.”

Ruling:
Overruled. One more hour of sleep will help more.

Practice:
At midnight, whisper: *“This brief can rest.”*
Close the file. Trust your earlier self.

Verdict:
Good work requires rest-both document and drafter.

Ruling No. 24: One Breath, One Choice.

Life feels overwhelming in bulk: cases, deadlines, demands. But it's lived moment by moment-one breath, one choice at a time. When panic hits, my breath shortens. When I slow it, clarity returns. I don't need the full solution, just the next sane decision.

Finding of Fact:

The next right choice is sufficient for today's ruling.

Objection:

"The system depends on me."

Ruling:

Overruled. The system depends on steps, not superheroes.

Practice:

When overwhelmed, take one deep breath and whisper:
"One breath, one choice." Then act on the smallest next thing.

Verdict:

You don't need the whole plan. Just the next move.

Ruling No. 25: Enough Already.
Sometimes, no metaphor. No eloquence. Just stop. Enough already. When my brain won't shut up 2 a.m. arguments, meeting over-explanations, family debates that spiral. I whisper it….*enough already.* It works like a gavel.

Finding of Fact:
The simplest rulings are often the truest.

Objection:
"But what if it's not enough yet?"

Ruling:
Overruled. If you're asking, it is.

Practice:
When you catch yourself spinning, say it aloud. *"Enough already."* Close the file. Walk away. Breathe.

Verdict:
Sometimes the gavel just needs to fall.

10 MICRO PRACTICES

for Daily Life

These are your small rulings-practical drills for letting go in real time. Each one is designed like a motion practice: short, actionable, and binding once filed. Use them daily. They'll retrain the lawyer brain faster than any verdict ever could.

1. The Inbox Audit
2. The Silent Pause
3. The Jurisdiction Test
4. The One-Minute Rule
5. The Enough Check
6. The Counsel Pause
7. The Achievement Fast
8. The Evening Check-In
9. The Tilt Test
10. The Surrender List

Micro-Practice No. 1: The Inbox Audit

Context

For lawyers, the inbox isn't a tool; it's a courtroom. Every ping is a filing, every "urgent" subject line a motion demanding immediate response. But most emails are noise disguised as necessity.

Evidence / Memoir

I once missed half my daughter's basketball game for an email labeled *URGENT.* I paced outside the gym, drafting a perfect response. The next day the client wrote, *"Thanks, noted."* They hadn't even read it until lunch. The emergency wasn't in my inbox, it was in my absence.

Quick Practice

Before replying, ask: *Does this require me?*
If not, archive it. If maybe, wait an hour.
If yes, reply with clarity, not speed.

Advanced Practice

Set two email windows daily. Outside them, close the app. Require calls for true emergencies. Watch how quickly "urgent" loses its footing.

Pitfalls

- Sending "Thanks" emails to feel polite.
- Letting email fill every pause in your day.
- Confusing responsiveness with reliability.

Verdict

Email is evidence, not oxygen. Every message you don't instantly answer is a quiet act of liberation.

Micro-Practice No. 2: The Silent Pause

Context

We're trained to fill silence with words-arguments, analysis, reassurance. But silence is leverage. Silence is presence. It's where clarity gathers its breath.

Evidence / Memoir

In a settlement conference, opposing counsel made a demand and stared me down. I paused-fifteen long seconds. He dropped his number without me saying a word. At home, my teenage son raged about curfew. I nearly lectured. Instead, I waited. The pause outlasted his anger. Connection won.

Quick Practice

Take one full breath before replying to anything that spikes your pulse.

Advanced Practice

Each day, practice three minutes of listening without interruption. In negotiations, let the silence stretch beyond comfort-you'll be amazed what fills it.

Pitfalls

- Mistaking silence for disengagement.
- Weaponizing silence to punish.
- Breaking it too soon.

Verdict

The pause is not absence-it's strategy. It replaces reaction with reason.

Micro-Practice No. 3: The Jurisdiction Test

Context
We know jurisdiction defines authority. Yet we act like we have global reach over people's moods, markets, and weather patterns.

Evidence / Memoir
I once stayed awake parsing a stock-market drop as if anxiety could alter the Dow. It didn't. I was practicing law outside my jurisdiction.

Quick Practice
When stressed, ask: *Is this mine to fix?* If not, dismiss it.

Advanced Practice
Each Sunday, make two columns-*Within My Control* (preparation, effort, presence) and *Outside My Control* (others' reactions, world events). Cross out the latter.

Pitfalls

- Confusing caring with controlling.
- Assuming influence equals authority.

Verdict
You lack universal jurisdiction. Close the cases you were never meant to hear.

Micro-Practice No. 4: The One-Minute Rule

Context

Most professional fires are started by lawyers who respond too fast.

Evidence / Memoir

A colleague once sent a snide midnight email. My fingers flew. For once, I waited one minute. The next morning, I rewrote the reply calmly. The minute saved the relationship, and my reputation.

Quick Practice

When triggered, wait sixty seconds. No exceptions.

Advanced Practice

Draft the fiery response, save it, reread it tomorrow. Ninety percent of the time, it'll self-destruct in daylight.

Pitfalls

- Confusing pause with avoidance.
- Letting the minute stretch into neglect.

Verdict

Most flames burn out in under a minute. Let them.

Micro-Practice No. 5: The Enough Check

Context

The finish line in law is a mirage. Partner, GC, board seat-each "arrival" just moves the goalpost. Enough is not found; it's declared.

Evidence / Memoir

When I reached the C-suite, I expected peace. Instead, I felt emptier. The title changed. The chase didn't.

Quick Practice

At day's end, ask: *What was enough today?*

Advanced Practice

Keep a thirty-day "enough log." Review monthly. You'll start noticing the moments that actually matter.

Pitfalls

- Defining enough only through achievement.
- Mistaking enough for mediocrity.

Verdict

Enough isn't laziness, it's jurisdictional clarity for your ambition.

Micro-Practice No. 6: The Counsel Pause

Context

Our title-*Counsel*-is occupational hazard. We drag it home, into friendships and family life, cross-examining loved ones under the guise of helping.

Evidence / Memoir

My partner came home upset. Within two minutes, I'd built a strategy deck in my head. She stopped me mid-sentence: "I don't need solutions. I need you to listen." Objection sustained.

Quick Practice

When someone vents, ask: *Do you want advice or empathy?* Then honor the answer.

Advanced Practice

Commit to one full conversation daily where you only listen, no fixes, no advice, no interruptions.

Pitfalls

- Sneaking advice in disguised as empathy.
- Confusing silence with uselessness.

Verdict

Not every problem requires counsel. Sometimes presence is the best representation.

Micro-Practice No. 7: The Achievement Fast

Context

Achievement is our drug of choice-billable, measurable, addictive. The achievement fast is rehab.

Evidence / Memoir

After closing a major deal, my instinct was to blast the announcement. Instead, I stayed silent. The itch for applause was real-but temporary. The satisfaction that followed was quieter, stronger.

Quick Practice

For one week, announce no wins. No humble-brags.
No "just sharing some exciting news."

Advanced Practice

Replace it with a daily "quiet win" unrelated to work-walking outside, cooking dinner, calling a friend. Record those for a month.

Pitfalls

Mistaking silence for invisibility.
Chasing external validation through "humility theater."

Verdict

Achievement is sweetest when it doesn't need an audience.

Micro-Practice No. 8: The Evening Check-In

Context

Lawyers end the day the same way we run it-unfinished. The evening check-in is your closing argument before sleep.

Evidence / Memoir

I used to scroll through emails until midnight, my mind still litigating tomorrow. Now I end each day by asking: *Where did I cling? Where did I let go?* Three minutes, two questions, total shift.

Quick Practice

Ask those two questions aloud before bed.

Advanced Practice

Journal the answers nightly for thirty days. You'll start spotting your patterns of peace and pressure.

Pitfalls

- Turning reflection into self-prosecution.
- Forgetting to celebrate the letting go.

Verdict

Closure invites rest. Rest restores judgment. Case closed.

Micro-Practice No. 9: The Tilt Test

Context

Balance is a myth perpetuated by burnout survivors. Life doesn't balance-it tilts. The goal isn't symmetry; it's honesty.

Evidence / Memoir

One week, I worked fourteen-hour days for trial prep. The next, I left early to help coach soccer. Neither was balanced. Both were right.

Quick Practice

Each Sunday, ask: *Where must I tilt this week-work, family, or rest?*

Advanced Practice

Share your tilt with someone you trust. Accountability keeps guilt at bay.

Pitfalls

- Trying to tilt everywhere.
- Apologizing for prioritizing.

Verdict

Stop chasing balance. Tilt with intention.

Micro-Practice No. 10: The Surrender List

Context

Lawyers grip everything-client moods, court rulings, the global economy. The surrender list is a written release of claims you never had standing to pursue.

Evidence / Memoir

During a deal, I obsessed over how analysts might react. My mentor said, "Write it down and cross it out." I did. My shoulders dropped. The anxiety didn't vanish-it lost authority.

Quick Practice

Each morning, write one thing you can't control today.
Cross it out.

Advanced Practice

Keep a weekly list. Read it aloud Friday evening, then shred it.

Pitfalls

- Treating surrender as defeat instead of wisdom.
- Re-litigating items you've already dismissed.

Verdict

Surrender isn't giving up. It's recusing yourself from cases outside your jurisdiction.

7 JOURNALING PROMPTS

Lawyers write for everyone else-judges, clients, partners, opposing counsel. Rarely do we write for ourselves. Journaling changes that. It's not about eloquence, grammar, or word count. It's about evidence. Discovery. The cross-examination of your own mind. These prompts are not essays to perfect. They are doorways. Each one asks you to look at what you're carrying, what you're clinging to, and what you're ready to release. You don't need long answers. Just honest ones.

Prompt No. 1: What Am I Carrying That Isn't Mine?

Context

Lawyers absorb everything. Clients hand us their panic. Partners hand us their urgency. Families hand us their hopes and fears. Eventually, we can't tell which burdens belong to us and which we've accidentally adopted.

Reflection

Think of a time you felt crushed by obligation. List every weight you're carrying-professional and personal. Then circle what actually belongs to you and cross out what doesn't.

Journal Practice

Write three things you're carrying right now that aren't yours. Notice how your body feels when you see them on paper. That physical exhale is evidence of release.

Example

I once lost sleep over whether a client CEO would fire her CFO. That wasn't my case. It wasn't even my call. The moment I labeled it "not mine," the weight lifted.

Prompt No. 2: Where in My Life Do I Confuse Control with Safety?

Context

We equate control with security: if I anticipate everything, I'll stay safe. If I manage every variable, no one will get hurt. But control doesn't create safety-it manufactures anxiety.

Reflection

Where do you mistake micromanagement for protection? At work? At home? In your relationships?

Journal Practice

Describe one situation where you cling to control. Then ask: *What would safety look like if I loosened my grip?*

Example

For years, I triple-checked every detail of my kids' weekend schedules-meals, carpools, sunscreen-as if precision guaranteed peace. All it did was make me tense. Presence was the safety I'd been chasing through control.

Prompt No. 3: What Belief About Myself Am I Ready to Rewrite?

Context
We live by invisible scripts-beliefs that once kept us safe but now keep us small. They whisper: "I'm not enough." "I have to fix everything." "I can't rest." We follow them without question, like outdated statutes no one's bothered to repeal.

Reflection
Which belief surfaces when you're overwhelmed or afraid?

Journal Practice
Write your old belief as if it's a line in a contract. Then strike it and draft a new clause. Read it aloud. See how your body reacts. That reaction is the truth.

Example
For years, mine was:
"If I don't hold it all together, everything falls apart."

I eventually replaced it with:
"I can be steady without being responsible for everything."

The rewrite changed everything.

Prompt No. 4: What Does Enough Look Like Today?

Context

Enough is the moving target of this profession. Every victory resets the bar. Every achievement becomes precedent for more. But "enough" isn't found in milestones-it's declared in moments.

Reflection

What would enough look like today-not in theory, but in this exact season of your life?

Journal Practice

Write three sentences starting with, *"Enough today is…"* Then keep your word to yourself.

Example

One Tuesday, enough was leaving the office at six, eating pizza with my kids, and watching a movie. Nothing billable. Everything valuable.

Prompt No. 5: If I Stopped Comparing, How Would I Measure My Life?

Context

Comparison is a courtroom we enter voluntarily-and we never win. Someone will always appear richer, younger, or more "together." But comparison uses someone else's facts to decide your case.

Reflection

If comparison disappeared, how would you measure your life? By peace? By presence? By laughter?

Journal Practice

List three personal metrics that matter more than competition. Then measure yourself by those-no appeal necessary.

Example

At a law school reunion, I quietly ranked my classmates by success. Later, one told me he envied my family life. Both of us were comparing, neither of us content.

Prompt No. 6: Where Did I Practice Surrender This Week?

Context
Surrender isn't quitting-it's realism. It's the moment you stop arguing with what's already true. Naming those moments reminds you that letting go is an act of strength, not weakness.

Reflection
In the past seven days, where did you stop fighting the uncontrollable?

Journal Practice
Write one instance of surrender this week. Then note how your body felt after. The calm is your evidence of power.

Example
During a volatile transaction, I stopped checking the market every hour. I finally said aloud, "That's not mine." Peace entered like oxygen.

Prompt No. 7: What Story Am I Still Telling That No Longer Fits?

Context
We all cling to outdated narratives: *I'm the fixer. The overachiever. The one who never rests.* They served us once. Now they suffocate us.

Reflection
Which story are you still telling out of habit or fear? What does it cost you to keep it alive?

Journal Practice
Write your old story in one paragraph. Cross it out. Then write the opening line of a new one-something more honest, more humane, more current. You're the author now.

Example
My story used to be:
"If I don't outwork everyone, I'll be forgotten."
At 25, it fueled me. At 45, it nearly broke me.

THE DAILY DOCKET

Lawyers respect structure. We trust dockets because they organize chaos. Hearings get set, motions get tracked, deadlines get met. But when it comes to our inner lives, we file nothing. We let thoughts, worries, and emotions pile up without order or closure.

The Daily Docket is how you apply your professional discipline to your personal peace. It's not another productivity hack, it's emotional case management.

A simple way to open and close each day with intention.The docket has two daily hearings, *Morning* and *Evening*, and one *Weekly Review.*

Each is short, structured, and sacred. Because when you treat your peace like a matter on the calendar, you stop losing track of it.

The Morning Docket

Start your day by clarifying three things:

- What I can control today
- What I cannot control today
- What I will consciously let go of today

That's it. By naming them, you give your mind a roadmap. This takes five minutes. Less time than scrolling headlines.

Example Morning Docket:

I can control:

- My preparation for the client call
- My tone in the team meeting
- Taking a walk at lunch

I cannot control:

- The partner's mood
- The client's decision
- The market reaction

I will let go:

- Obsessing about the board chair's opinion of me

The Evening Docket

End your day by answering three prompts:

- What I carried today
- What I dropped today
- Where I found peace today

It forces you to notice-not just the burdens but the victories of release. Writing this down trains your brain to acknowledge letting go as progress.

Example Evening Docket:

- ***I carried:*** My team's deadline stress
- ***I dropped:*** Responding to two non-urgent emails
- ***I found peace:*** Laughing with my kids over dinner

The Weekly Review

Lawyers love reviewing case files. Apply the same rigor to your week. On Friday afternoon, take 10 minutes to ask:

- Where did urgency steal my time?
- Where did presence return it?
- What will I do differently next week?

Why it Works
The Daily Docket externalizes what otherwise clogs your brain. It's like filing motions: once it's on the record, you don't have to hold it all in your head. The brain craves closure. The docket gives it.

Verdict
You can't control the system, but you can run your own docket. Morning, evening, and weekly, three check-ins to keep peace on the calendar.

Sample Weekly Review

- Urgency stole my time: *Jumping into a pointless "urgent" email chain*

- Presence returned it: *Taking Wednesday off my phone for two hours.*

- Next week: *Block 30 minutes daily for real work, not inbox triage.*

THE EMERGENCY TOOLKIT

MOTION

The Five Breath Reset

Context:

Your nervous system is the first thing to hijack you. Breath brings it back.

How it Works:

Inhale for 4, hold for 4, exhale for 4, hold for 4. Repeat five times.

Memoir:

I've done this in courthouse bathrooms, boardroom hallways, even in my parked car outside a deposition. Each time, my pulse slowed, my thoughts cleared, and I remembered I wasn't about to die, I was just anxious.

Practice:

When panic spikes, excuse yourself if needed. Five breaths. Nothing more.

Verdict:

It's the quickest reset you can carry anywhere.

MOTION
The Walkout

Context:
Staying in the same room keeps you stuck in the same loop.

How it Works:
Change the room, change the state. Stand up. Walk out. Two minutes is enough.

Memoir:
Once in a contentious negotiation, I excused myself "to grab water." That two-minute hallway walk broke the cycle. I returned calm. The deal closed.

Practice:
When stuck, walk out, even if it's just to the restroom. Reset the scene.

Verdict:
Movement breaks momentum.

MOTION
The Gratitude Docket

Context:
Anxiety narrows focus to everything going wrong. Gratitude widens the lens.

How it Works:
List three things going right, out loud.

Memoir:
After a brutal hearing, I sat in my car and forced myself: "I have a job. I have a family. I have another chance tomorrow." My mood softened.

Practice:
Say it aloud. Not in your head. Hearing it matters.

Verdict:
Gratitude doesn't erase stress. It balances the record.

MOTION

5,4,3,2,1 Grounding Drill

Context:
Anxiety drags you into “what if.” This drill drags you back into “what is.”

How it Works:
Name 5 things you see, 4 things you feel, 3 things you hear, 2 things you smell, 1 thing you taste.

Memoir:
Before a closing argument, I felt the spiral coming. My chest was tight, my head buzzing. I did this drill silently at counsel table. By the time I reached “taste,” I was steady.

Practice:
Do it anywhere a desk, train, courtroom. This re-anchors you to the present.

Verdict:
Reality is calmer than imagination.

MOTION TO DISMISS

Not-My-Job List

Context:
We hoard responsibilities that don't belong to us. This tool names and dismisses them.

How it Works:
Write down everything you're carrying. Circle what's yours. Cross out what isn't.

Memoir:
I once lost sleep over whether a colleague would file an appellate on time. It wasn't mine. Writing it down and crossing it off freed me to rest.

Practice:
Keep a scrap sheet handy. Label "Mine" and "Not Mine." Rip up the latter.

Verdict:
You don't have to try every case.

MOTION

One-Minute Silence

Context:
We fill silence with words, screens, noise. But silence restores equilibrium.

How it Works:
Sit with no phone, no agenda, no words. One minute.

Memoir:
Before board presentations, I used to scroll through my email and Slack frantically. Then I tried one minute of silence instead. I walked in clearer.

Practice:
Set a timer. Sixty seconds. Nothing but breath.

Verdict:
Silence isn't absence. It's medicine.

MOTION
The Hand Drop

Context:
Sometimes you need a physical symbol of surrender.

How it Works:
Pick up an object. Grip it tightly. Then, open your hand and let it fall.
Notice the release. That's surrender.
No speech. No drama. Just release.

Memoir:
I've dropped pens in chambers, stress balls in my office, even my phone (carefully). Each time, my body felt the metaphor: you can let go.

Practice:
When you feel clenched, grab what is near. Drop it. Watch gravity do what you cannot.

Verdict:
Letting go isn't dramatic. It's a hand opening.

MOTION
Cold Water Reset

Context:
Shock interrupts spirals.

How it Works:
Splash cold water on your face or run wrists under a cold tap.

Memoir:
Before depositions, I’ve locked myself in restrooms to do this. Walking out, my system was calmer, my head clearer.

Practice:
Next time you’re spinning, find a sink. Use the water.

Verdict:
Cold water is the cheapest therapy you’ll ever find.

MOTION
The Bench Trial

Context:
We keep appealing reality, as if more argument will change it. The Bench Trial makes you rule on the facts.

How it Works:
Say: “This is reality. I don’t have to like it. But I accept it.”

Memoir:
When a judge ruled against me on a motion I thought I’d win, I stewed for days. Finally, I whispered this to myself. The ruling didn’t change, but my fight against it stopped.

Practice:
Use it when replaying something you can’t alter. Accept the record.

Verdict:
Acceptance is not approval. It’s closure.

EMERGENCY STIPULATION

The Three Sentence Prayer

Context:
When all else fails, words can anchor you.

How it Works:
Say aloud, “I’m here. That’s enough. Begin again.”

Memoir:
I’ve said this in bathrooms, cars, even walking into court. Each time, it steadied me.

Practice:
Memorize it. Use it whenever you’re lost.

Verdict:
Sometimes three sentences are all you need.

THE CONSENT DECREE

A 30-Day Plan for Letting Go

This plan isn't about perfection. It's about practice. Thirty days of small, intentional acts that retrain your lawyer brain to un-clench. Each day has a focus, a practice, and a reflection. Follow in sequence or pick the ones that call to you.

BOUNDARIES [DAYS 1 – 7]

DAY 1: Inbox Audit
Focus: Notice email is not your master.
Practice: Leave 3 non-urgent emails unanswered for 24-hrs.

Reflection:
Did anything collapse? Or did silence serve?

DAY 2: Say 'No' Once
Focus: Boundaries create freedom.
Practice: Decline one request without over-explaining.
Just say: *"I can't take this on right now."*

Reflection:
How much discomfort did you feel? How much relief?

DAY 3: The Jurisdiction Test
Focus: You don't control everything.
Practice: Write down 5 worries. Circle what's yours. Cross out the rest.

Reflection:
What dropped off your shoulders?

DAY 4: The Tilt Test
Focus: Life tilts, not balances.
Practice: Decide this week, will you tilt toward work, family, or rest? Tell someone.

Reflection:
Did declaring it make you feel guilty or free?

DAY 5: The Evening Check-In
Focus: Closure matters.
Practice: Write, Where did I cling today? Where did I let go?

Reflection:
What patterns are emerging?

DAY 6: Objection Journal
Focus: Anticipate resistance.
Practice: Write down every objection your inner critic raises today. Answer them like opposing counsel.

Reflection:
How persuasive is your critic, really?

DAY 7: Weekly Review
Focus: Summarize the week.
Practice: Ask, where did urgency steal my time?
Where did presence return it?

Reflection:
What one adjustment matters most next week?

PRESENCE [DAYS 8 – 14]

DAY 8: The Silent Pause
Focus: Slow down reactivity.
Practice: Take one breath before speaking or replying.

Reflection:
How did silence shift the outcome?

DAY 9: The Three-Minute Drill
Focus: Listen, don't fix.
Practice: Spend three minutes listening without interrupting or offering solutions.

Reflection:
How did it change the conversation?

DAY 10: Imperfect Email
Focus: Excellence, not perfection.
Practice: Send one email today without rereading it five times.

Reflection:
Did the world end? Or did it save you time?

DAY 11: The One-Minute Rule
Focus: Delay reaction.
Practice: When triggered, wait 60 seconds before replying.

Reflection:
Did the urge shift?

DAY 12: The Walkout
Focus: Change the room, change the state.
Practice: Step outside for five-minutes during a stressful moment.

Reflection:
How did your body respond?

DAY 13: The Hand Drop
Focus: Surrender in action.
Practice: Grip an object, then drop it.
Say: "*I release this.*"

Reflection:
What did your body feel?

DAY 14: Gratitude Docket
Focus: Balance the record.
Practice: List three things that went right today. Out loud.

Reflection:
Did gratitude change the narrative of your day?

IDENTITY [DAYS 15 – 21]

DAY 15: The Worth Audit
Focus: Separate worth from wins.
Practice: List 5 qualities that make you valuable beyond work.

Reflection:
Which felt hardest to name?

DAY 16: Achievement Fast
Focus: Break dependence on applause.
Practice: Go one day without announcing a win. Keep it to yourself.

Reflection:
Did silence make you invisible or lighter?

DAY 17: Rewrite the Narrative
Focus: Update your self-story.
Practice: Write an old script you live by. Cross it out. Write a new one.

Reflection:
Which feels more like you?

DAY 18: Presence over Perfection
Focus: Show up messy.
Practice: Enter one meeting or conversation without over-preparing. Just be there.

Reflection:
Did anyone notice your imperfections?

DAY 19: Comparison Cross-Examination
Focus: See through illusions.
Practice: Pick one post that triggers envy. Cross-examine it. What facts are missing? What spin is here?

Reflection:
How persuasive was the evidence?

DAY 20: The Enough Check
Focus: Declare sufficiency.
Practice: Write one sentence.
"Enough. Today is…"

Reflection:
How did naming enough shift your day?

DAY 21: The Surrender List
Focus: Set down what isn't yours.
Practice: Write one uncontrollable thing. Cross it out.

Reflection:
Did your body release even slightly?

SURRENDER [DAYS 22 – 30]

DAY 22: Bench Trial
Focus: Accept reality.
Practice: Say aloud, "This is reality. I don't have to like it, but I accept it."

Reflection:
Did naming reality change your fight against it?

DAY 23: Cold-Water Reset
Focus: Shock interrupts spirals.
Practice: Splash cold water on your face or wrists when feeling anxious or stressed.

Reflection:
Did the shock bring you back?

DAY 24: Daily Docket for Peace
Focus: Structure peace.
Practice: Fill out morning and evening dockets.

Reflection:
What clarity came from writing?

DAY 25: Redefine the Win
Focus: Quiet victories matter.
Practice: Choose one non-work win today; cooking, rest, laughter. Celebrate it.

Reflection:
Did redefining success expand your sense of value?

DAY 26: Five-Breath Reset
Focus: Calm the nervous system.
Practice: Inhale 4. Hold 4. Exhale 4. Hold 4. 5 times.

Reflection:
How different did you feel after two minutes?

DAY 27: Someday Inventory
Focus: Stop deferring life.
Practice: Write 5 things you've been saving for "someday." Circle one. Do it today!

Reflection:
What kept you waiting?

DAY 28: Draft Your Peace Clause
Focus: Write your own contract.
Practice: Draft one binding clause, e.g., "I will not tie my worth to productivity." Sign it.

Reflection:
Did it feel silly or freeing?

DAY 29: Choose One Mantra
Focus: Repetition rewires.
Practice: Pick one mantra. Repeat it all day.

Reflection:
How did it shape your choices?

DAY 30: Closing Argument to Yourself
Focus: Summarize the case for peace.
Practice: Write a one-page closing statement. What you've learned. What you're letting go. What you'll carry forward.

Reflection:
How did it feel to advocate for yourself?

CLOSING

Thirty days won't erase years or decades of habits. But thirty days can remind you: you are not powerless. Each practice is a retraining. Each reflection is a redirect.

You don't have to hold the whole system.
You don't have to be perfect.
You don't have to wait for someday.

You can let go—one day, one breath, and one choice at a time.

DRAFTING YOUR PEACE CLAUSE

Lawyers live by contracts. Every deal, every clause, every signature represents clarity who owes what, what happens if there's a breach, what protection exists when things fall apart. We draft those documents for everyone else. But most of us go through life without ever drafting one for ourselves. We live under silent, outdated agreements written decades ago:

- *I will always be the fixer.*
- *I must be perfect to be loved.*
- *My worth is tied to my wins.*

They were never negotiated. Never signed. But they've ruled our lives like implied covenants.

It's time to draft a new one. A peace clause.

Why a Peace Clause Matters

A peace clause isn't an escape hatch. It's not a loophole in the contract of your life. It's a declaration of terms that protect your humanity.

Just as you negotiate indemnification clauses to protect your clients, you can draft a peace clause to protect yourself.

Without one, you'll keep living under invisible obligations:

- to respond instantly
- to overdeliver
- to prove your worth in every room

With one, you'll have a binding document, written by you, for you, that reminds you where your true duties end and your peace begins.

My First Peace Clause

Mine was drafted during a season of collapse, the kind where you can't tell if you're tired or just done.

In a journal, I wrote:
"I will not confuse productivity with worth.
I am allowed to rest.
I am allowed to be imperfect.
I am allowed to be human."

It felt embarrassingly simple. But that paragraph became a precedent. Each time I felt the old reflexes, another midnight email, another self-imposed trial. I returned to that clause. It was my personal indemnity provision against burnout.

How to Draft Yours

1. Identify the Old Contract
Write down one unspoken rule that's been running your life.

Example: *If I don't hold it all together, everything will fall apart.*

2. Name the Harm
Ask: *How has this clause damaged me?*
Maybe it's cost you sleep, strained relationships, or buried your joy.

3. Redraft in Favor of Peace
Write a new clause that restores sanity.

Example: *I can be steady without carrying everything. I can trust others. I can rest without guilt.*

4. Make It Binding
Sign it. Date it. Post it.
Treat it like a legal instrument, because it is. You're entering a contract with yourself, enforceable by compassion.

Prompts for Your Peace Clause

Use these to shape your new terms:

- *"I will not..."* (what you're releasing)
- *"I will..."* (what you're choosing to honor)
- *"I choose..."* (your new posture)
- *"I accept..."* (the reality you're no longer resisting)

Examples:

- *"I will not tie my worth to billable hours."*
- *"I will choose presence over polish."*
- *"I accept that I cannot control outcomes."*
- *"I choose to rest without apology."*

Each statement is a clause
in the contract of your own peace.

PEACE CLAUSE CASE STUDIES

ASSOCIATE LEVEL

A junior lawyer wrote:
*"I will not equate silence from partners with failure.
I will assume neutrality until told otherwise."*

That one clause cut her anxiety in half.

PARTNER LEVEL

A partner drafted:
*"I will not micromanage to prove my value. I will trust my team and measure success by outcomes,
not fingerprints."*

Morale went up. Turnover went down. So did his blood pressure.

PERSONAL LIFE

A parent wrote:
*"I will not measure my love by how much I provide.
I will measure it by presence."*

That clause changed more than their household. It changed their posture toward life.

Enforcement

Contracts need remedies. So does this one. When you breach your peace clause, and you will — don't default to punishment. Default to renewal.

If you catch yourself at midnight violating your own terms, pause.

Whisper: *"Breach cured."*
Close the laptop. Begin again.

Advanced Practice: The Living Contract

Like any good agreement, your peace clause can evolve. What protects you now may not serve you five years from now. Revisit it quarterly.

Ask: *Does this clause still safeguard my peace?*
Does it need to be amended?

Peace is a living document. So are you.

My Current Peace Clause
"I will not confuse exhaustion with excellence.
I will honor effort, not outcome.
I will surrender what isn't mine.
I will choose peace, daily, even when the system
tells me otherwise."

It doesn't guarantee peace every day. But it gives me boundaries, language, and a framework - a contract I chose, not one inherited from fear.

CLOSING ARGUMENT

You've spent your career drafting contracts for others. Now it's your turn. Write one for yourself.

Sign it with conviction. Post it where you'll see it when the noise gets loud. Because if you don't, the world will write one for you, and it will not be kind.

Without a peace clause, you live by someone else's terms. With one, you reclaim authorship of your own.

Peace isn't a loophole.
It's binding precedent.

PART VII

The Verdict Form

VERDICT FORM

In the matter of: Carrying the Whole System
Jurisdiction: The Court of My Own Life

FINDINGS OF FACT

Having reviewed the evidence of my own life, I find the following to be true:

- Exhaustion is not excellence.
- Perfection is not professionalism.
- Control is not safety.
- My self-worth is not on trial.
- Peace is admissible.

VERDICT

- I cannot carry the whole system.
- I can only carry my part.
- I choose to release what is not mine.
- I will practice letting go daily, I can always begin again.

JUDGEMENT

Accordingly, I render judgment in favor of:

- Presence over polish.
- Peace over performance.
- Humanity over machine.

SIGNATURE

I hereby enter this verdict into the permanent record of my life.

Date:______________

Signature:______________________________

Print Name:______________________________

ACKNOWLEDGEMENTS

Writing this book has been a long, winding process that mirrors the work inside it: *letting go, loosening the grip, and learning to carry only what's mine.* I'm grateful to everyone who helped me along the way. Especially those who loved and supported me at my worst and helped me get up and keep going each time I fell. Thank you, Luca, Gemma, Bella, Neeley, Mom, Dad, Rob, and Mike.

Thank you to the mentors, colleagues, and leaders who taught me the craft of law and the discipline of professional detachment, sometimes by showing me what to do, and other times by showing me exactly what not to do. To the teams I've led and the teams I've learned from: *you shaped this book more than you know.*

To my family: each of you has been a lighthouse for me in your own way, guiding me through different darknesses with an unconditional steadiness that never wavered, even in seasons of my painful imperfection. I wouldn't have found my way without your light.

And to every lawyer who feels tired, responsible for everything, or trapped by their own standards: I hope these pages make you feel less alone, and remind you that letting go isn't giving up. It's finally coming up for air.

ABOUT THE AUTHOR

Matthew Campobasso has spent nearly two decades practicing law at the intersection of business, leadership, and human behavior. As a seasoned General Counsel and Chief Legal Officer with experience in both public and private company leadership, he has advised CEOs, boards, founders, and operators through moments of extreme pressure—IPOs, take-privates, restructurings, investigations, crises, and the quiet daily grind of sound decision-making.

Over those years, he recognized a pattern: the legal profession rewards over-control, chronic responsibility, and self-sacrifice until the bill comes due. Early in his career, Matt believed what most lawyers are taught to believe: *that the only way to succeed is to work harder, care more, and keep everything under control.* The results were predictable success on paper, exhaustion in practice.

As his teams grew and his scope widened, he noticed something unsettling: brilliant lawyers were burning out, not because they lacked talent or intelligence, but because they were carrying weight that didn't belong to them.

That realization led him toward emotional detachment—not the cold, clinical kind, but the disciplined, professional kind. A deliberate loosening of the grip. A shift from *"I must fix everything"* to *"I will do excellent work on what's mine and let the rest be."*

Matt's work blends Stoic philosophy, therapy, modern behavioral science, and the lived experience of leading legal teams through real-world pressure. He teaches that detachment is not indifference; it's competence. It's not lowering your standards; it's lowering your self-destruction. His writing aims to help lawyers, and anyone who thinks like one to reclaim a sense of agency, calm, and humanity in a profession that rarely pauses to breathe.

When he's not working or writing, Matt is a dad trying to keep up with three incredible kids: Luca, Gemma, and Bella. His interests run wide: Stoicism, film, music, meditation, and whatever else helps him make sense of the chaos. Above all, Matt is a work in progress. '*The Case for Letting Go*' is his honest argument for a saner, more sustainable path forward in a profession he loves.

Thank You for Reading

The right book at the right moment can change everything. If this was that book for you, passing it forward is as simple as leaving a review. It only takes a minute, and it might be exactly what the next reader needs to find."

Explore Our Catalog

BROOKLYN
WRITERS PRESS
AN IMPRINT OF ARIS PUBLISHING GROUP

brooklynwriterspress.com

www.ingramcontent.com/pod-product-compliance
Lightning Source LLC
Chambersburg PA
CBHW031337230926
51848CB00002B/280
9781952991578